Teaching with Google Jamboard

50+ Ways to Use the Digital Whiteboarding Tool

Alice Keeler + Kimberly Mattina

Teaching with Google Jamboard: 50+ Ways to Use the Digital Whiteboarding Tool
©2021 Alice Keeler and Kimberly Mattina

This book is available at special discounts when purchased in quantity for educational purposes or for use as premiums, promotions, or fundraisers. For inquiries and details, contact the publisher at books@daveburgessconsulting.com.

Published by Dave Burgess Consulting, Inc.
San Diego, CA
DaveBurgessConsulting.com

Library of Congress Control Number: 2021938167
Paperback ISBN: 978-1-951600-85-3
E-book ISBN: 978-1-951600-86-0

Cover and interior design by Liz Schreiter
Editing and production by Reading List Editorial: readinglisteditorial.com

Contents

Foreword

by Alexes M. Terry

Because my overall goal as an educator is to create equitable learning spaces where all students feel seen, heard, and empowered, I am always looking for new twists on the ways teaching and learning can happen. I'm constantly seeking out ways to allow my students to collaborate, create, and take control of what they learn, how they learn, and how they demonstrate mastery of what they learn. Jamboard helps me to do all of that.

Incorporating Jamboard into my lessons took student engagement to a new level. As we learned and played around with this amazing collaborative digital whiteboard, we kept finding new, transformative ways to use it to enhance and organize our discussions and other aspects of our class. We used Jamboard to connect trends in our learning, share new insights and resources about content, work on project-based lessons, and plan future learning—all collaboratively. Jamboard created a community in my classroom that allowed every student's voice to be heard, both when it came to their individual needs and our collective needs as a class. With Jamboard, everyone, including myself, had a space to share what was on their mind. Even when we were not physically in the same space, we could

keep our discussions, reflections, and connections going. Jamboard helped me identify students who needed more support to meet their individualized learning needs. And if there was something that needed to be addressed in the next class period, Jamboard allowed me to pick up right where we left off.

It is also a tool that can help teachers understand the importance of culture in the classroom (or school). To create academic spaces that effectively reach and teach all students, culturally responsive teaching and practices are a must. One of the biggest problems that exists in the field of education is educators who are committed to teaching students they don't know beyond the surface level things our eyes can see.

Before we design any lesson, plan out a classroom activity, or introduce our students to a digital tool, we must implement a continuous process of intentionally getting to know our students. Really knowing our students means going beyond an interest in their favorite foods or color. It's more than a familiarity with their pets, siblings, or even the holidays they enjoy celebrating with their families. Knowing that information is nice, but it will not get us far in building and sustaining the kind of trusting relationships with students necessary to create safe and inclusive learning spaces. The information that matters comes from knowing our students' cultures; learning about their communities; understanding what issues are important to them and their families; and being fully aware of how they authentically show up in our classrooms and what they need from us to exist as their authentic selves.

Teachers must fill their toolboxes with tools that are effective at reaching and teaching each individual student, while students fill their toolboxes with the knowledge, assets, and skills they will use to change their communities, the nation, and the world. Culturally responsive teachers use a multitude of tools to get to students' hearts, build them up, and create spaces for them to thrive. Jamboard has the flexibility to allow educators to get to know their students and the various ways they can affirm their students' identities, cultures, voices, and passions.

> **Tip**
> Use Jamboard frequently to amplify student voices and create inclusive learning opportunities that can affirm their cultural identities.

To create equitable spaces where all students can thrive, we must use instructional tools to create an environment where all students feel like valued members of a learning community and can take charge of their own learning and share their thoughts, ideas, and passions in meaningful ways. That's how we can ignite change. I saw Jamboard do this in my classroom, and it is my hope that the strategies shared in this book will empower you to use it in the same way as you get your Jam on with your students. I am excited to see Alice and Kimberly share so many different ways that other educators can use to see, hear, and empower their students with this powerful yet simple tool.

Alexes M. Terry is an educator, consultant, and founder of TwistED Teaching Educational Consulting Company. She is the author of the book *REAL LOVE: Strategies for Reaching Students when They See No Way Out.* With over a decade of experience, Alexes is always searching for new ways to transform learning experiences and opportunities for her students and support other educators in doing the same. She believes that education is freedom and making classrooms equitable is the start to creating an equitable world.

Introduction

Jamboard is a tool for collaborative digital whiteboarding. Learners and educators can use it together in order to sketch out their thinking, share ideas, add images, and draw, all from the ease of their own devices.

In this book, we'll highlight some of the ways that Jamboard can be a great tool for student learning for K–12 students in all subject areas. We will guide you through pedagogy and instruction and help you access dynamic learning materials that will allow you to interact with students and are accessible anytime, anywhere.

Why Google Jamboard?

When making a decision to use technology, there are some important questions that we have to ask: Why are we choosing a particular tool? How does it improve learning? Why is it better than another tool we could choose?

Each tool in the Google Workspace provides unique methods for improving the learning experience. Jamboard, Google's digital whiteboard app, stands out among them because of several advantages that make it an excellent choice for learning activities: You can use Jamboard to teach—dynamically—both in person and remotely. It is a great way for educators and students to express learning visually, allowing learning to be illustrated through the use of handwriting, drawings, images, charts, and much, much more. It's also available to use for free, and you can easily access Jamboard files right in Google Drive.

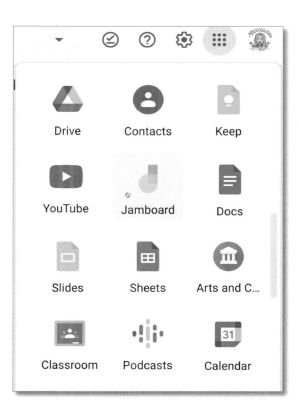

The biggest advantage that Google Workspace apps provide is real-time collaboration, and Jamboard is no exception. Jamboard can be used by multiple users at the same time. Its ability to enable students to learn together, whether they—or their teachers—are in person or remote, tremendously improves student engagement and learning.

Jams are free

NO PRESENT BUTTON

To really understand what Jamboard *is*, it's important to understand what it is *not*: There is no option to insert comments, like there is in Google Docs, Sheets, and Slides. That's because the entire purpose of Jamboard is to get people together and share ideas. No comment option is necessary; the whole space is a place to comment.

For the same reasons, Jamboard also does not have a present button. However, when students need to make formal presentations of the ideas and collaborations they've done in Jamboard, there is a way to export frames as images that can be added to Google Slides.

Three Ways to Jam

There is a lot of confusion with the terms around Jamboard. So let's clear that up. There is the Jamboard app, Jamboard on the Web, and the Jamboard Kiosk. Let's take a look at the differences.

This book will focus primarily on the web version of Jamboard. **The Kiosk is not required** to teach with Jamboard Jams. Since many schools have not made the leap to purchase physical Jamboard Kiosks, we will assume that you are using the **free** web version or the **free** app version and that students and teachers will be accessing the Jams through Chromebooks, computers, iPads, and/or mobile devices.

JAMBOARD ON THE WEB

Jamboard for the web is available for FREE through Google Drive. Once you start creating Jams, you will see them listed in Drive just like any other Google document. You can rename, move, and delete Jams just like any other Google document.

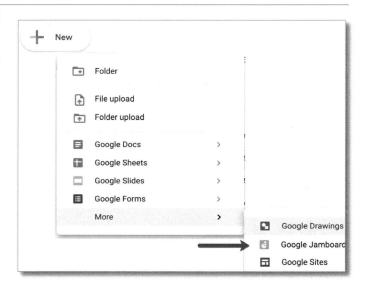

JAMBOARD APP

Just as Google Docs, Sheets, and Slides can be accessed on an iOS or Android device through an app rather than going through the

Safari or Chrome browsers, Jams, too, have their own dedicated app. While we often use Jamboard on a nontouchscreen device, a touchscreen Chromebook, PC, iPad, or mobile device can enhance the experience.

The Jamboard app is FREE and available at the Google Play and Apple Stores. It can be downloaded to mobile devices or tablets or installed on Chromebooks. The app can be installed through the Google Admin console and pushed out to multiple Chromebook devices managed by a school district. The same Jam can be open in the web version or the app version, allowing Chromebook users to toggle experiences. Even if you create Jams in the app, you will still see all of your Jams listed in Google Drive.

Like the apps for Google Docs, Google Sheets, and Google Slides, the Jamboard mobile app has different features than its web (or Kiosk) counterpart, starting with the collapsed controls, which allow for easier navigation on mobile devices.

TIP

It's best to use the latest version of Google Chrome to access Jamboard on the web.

TIP

It's best to install the latest version of the app on your mobile device. This will ensure that you are working with the most up-to-date and bug-free version.

The app also allows users to write words on the Jam using the **Assistive Drawing** tools for text. This automatically converts handwriting to typed text. (Handwriting created using the **Pen** tool will not convert to typed text; the user must use the **Assistive Drawing** tools.) **Assistive Drawing** tools for shapes are also available. For example, drawing a circle with the **Assistive Drawing** tool, rather than the **Pen** tool, will convert your shape into a perfect circle. This shape recognition is available for all basic shapes, like squares and triangles.

Sample Jam:
Unique Features
of the App

The magic of autodraw.com is built into the app (and the Kiosk). Autodraw in the app allows for fast drawing of almost anything! Again, you must use the **Assistive Drawing** tool—not the **Pen** tool—and autodraw will suggest a drawing and convert it.

App users are able to insert into Jamboard from Google Drive, and you can insert a particular slide from a Google Slides presentation or a page from a Google Doc. The Jamboard app also makes it easy to insert pictures directly from your mobile device. You can take a picture directly onto the Jam by using the **Insert menu** and choosing "Camera," or you can select one from the device's gallery.

THE JAMBOARD KIOSK

The Jamboard Kiosk is a physical device that can be placed in your classroom to help you interact and collaborate with students, whether you are in person or remote. It's a fifty-five-inch touchscreen device that can be mounted on the wall or placed on a separately purchased moveable stand. Typically you might have only one Jamboard Kiosk per classroom or share one between multiple rooms. It is not necessary to have a Kiosk to effectively teach with Jamboard, but the device can enhance the classroom experience.

The Jamboard Kiosk must be purchased from an **authorized dealer.** Education customers are charged a one-time (not annual) maintenance fee in addition to the cost of the device.

The Kiosk stands alone: No computer is required, and there is no software to install on a separate device. You are not hampered by having to hook it up to anything or know a login to start using it. You just turn it on and go!

The difference between creating a Jam on the web and creating a Jam on the Kiosk is ownership. Creating a Jam on the web automatically associates the Jam file with your Google Drive account. However, creating one from the Kiosk does not. This is an advantage. Jams created by students or visitors do not necessarily end up in your Google Drive, denying the creator access. However, if you'd like to automatically capture work in the Jamboard Kiosk to your Google Drive, you can choose to log in.

Student work is easily shared with the Kiosk.

Without having to sign into Jamboard, students can connect to the Kiosk from their seats, as long as they are on the same wifi network as the Kiosk. Many schools will create a separate wifi network just for Jamboard Kiosks.

A Jamboard Kiosk is NOT an interactive display tool. You can connect your computer to it to present your screen, however, the Jamboard Kiosk does not otherwise interact with your computer.

If you're interested in the Kiosk, we highly recommend the mobile stand. Getting the Kiosk off the wall allows you to move the class's focus away from the front of the room and help students present ideas anywhere.

Sample Jam:
Connect to Kiosk

Assistive drawing tools on the Kiosk are more robust than in the Jamboard app. In addition to handwriting recognition and shape recognition, the Kiosk also allows for the use of Autodraw. These tools can be found in the **Pen** tool menu.

Jamboard is integrated with Google Meet video conferencing, and using the Kiosk with Meet expands the possibilities for collaboration. A Meet conference can be created or joined right from the Kiosk, and the Jam will be associated with the conference. No computer or additional device is required. It is a great way to invite students to lessons if they're outside of the classroom.

Sample Jam:
Kiosk Assistive
Drawing Tools

The Lingo

Just like every new app, there are some key terms for Jamboard that you should be familiar with.

- **Jams** are the individual files that you create. They are stored in Google Drive.
- A **frame** is a page of a Jam.
- The **Frame Bar** is at the top center of the Jamboard interface, and it allows you to delete, duplicate, or move frames in the Jam.
- **Drawing strokes** are anything written on a frame with the **Pen** tool.
- **Assistive Drawing** tools, such as handwriting and shape recognition, are tools that transform your handwriting into printed text or basic shapes.
- The **Autodraw** tool provides suggestions for what you are drawing.

WHAT IS A JAM?

A new file in Jamboard is referred to as a Jam, and it is saved in Google Drive. Jams are just like documents in Google Docs, Google Sheets, and Google Slides, and they integrate seamlessly with these other applications. They can be shared the same way as Google Docs, and they can be added to Google Classroom or any learning management system.

Sample Jam:
Jamboard
Whiteboard
Get Started

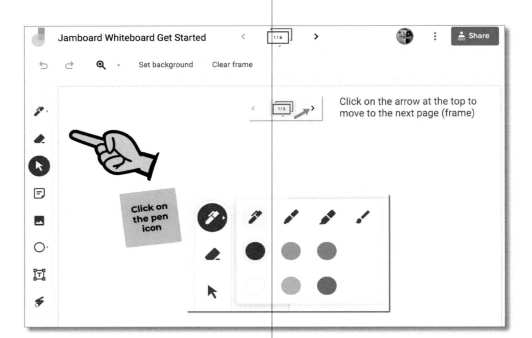

Digital Expectations

We recommend going over digital expectations with your students so they know how to behave and respect others while collaborating. Behaving well in a collaborative digital environment is a learned skill, just like behaving well in the library. Students need to learn that doing things like deleting or editing others' responses is not acceptable behavior. Having a set of rules and guidelines established prior to using Jamboard will help encourage good behavior.

Sample Jam:
Digital
Expectations

The 4 Cs

The 4 Cs of twenty-first century education are collaboration, communication, critical thinking, and creative thinking. It is important that every lesson has at least one of these elements. No tool provides these for you; educators must intentionally include them in lesson plans.

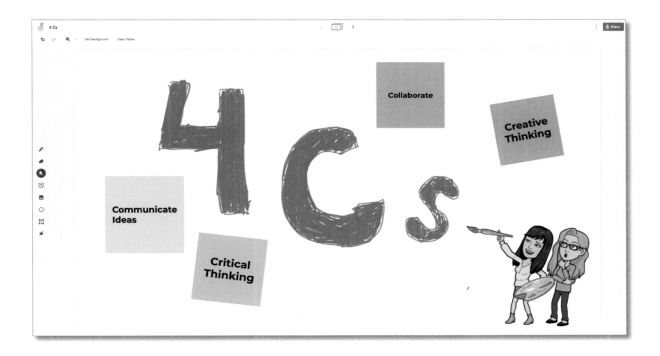

COLLABORATION

Jamboard is designed for collaboration. Any teacher looking to increase collaboration in the classroom should consider including Jams in their lesson design. It's possible to have multiple students work together on a single large sheet of chart paper, but this excludes any students who are not physically present. Then there's the challenge of where to store the work: there is limited wall space in a physical classroom for huge sheets of paper.

But classrooms in the twenty-first century are not limited to four walls, and technology should do more than replace paper. With Jamboard, every student can write on and interact with a collaborative project at the same time, even if they are not in the same room. In fact, its capabilities add new and improved ways of collaborating to the classroom. No longer is one student with the pen doing most of the work.

COMMUNICATION

Communication is more than talking. Students need to learn how to clearly communicate their ideas beyond just giving facts.

For example, a key for teaching math in the twentieth century was to ask students to "show your work." In the twenty-first century, this is obsolete. Technology has changed how we interact with the world. When students have phones in their pockets and use computers daily, many of the old skills that were once important have become unimportant. The PhotoMath app allows students to take a picture of a math problem and see the work step by step. Now, instead of the low-critical-thinking task of "showing your work," which can be done by computer, we ask math students to communicate their ideas.

Here are a few things we might ask students to do to communicate their learning about math concepts:

- Explain why a process works.
- How could it be applied to a unique situation?
- How can it be generalized?
- What happens if something is changed in a problem?
- What are the limitations of this process?
- What conditions are necessary for this formula to be used?
- Derive the formula (instead of using the formula).
- Prove the formula.
- Compare and contrast solutions from PhotoMath.
- How is this technique similar to other techniques you have used before?
- Now that you know you can solve problems in this way, can you think of other ways that would also work? How would you choose between these methods?

> Now, instead of the low-critical-thinking task of "showing your work," which can be done by computer, we ask math students to communicate their ideas.

CRITICAL THINKING

When designing lessons and activities, it is important to assess the critical thinking we are asking students to do. Then, we should strive to ask students to reach higher levels of critical thinking.

Depth of Knowledge, or DOK, was developed by Dr. Norman Webb as a measurement of the critical thinking levels a student is engaged in on a 4-point scale. It is common to utilize a DOK wheel of verbs to help aid in determining DOK level, but the verbs and the wheel by themselves are insufficient. Asking students to *create* something (like a Jam) will likely produce low critical thinking—unless the task requires that students extend their reasoning.

DOK 1 is memorization and recall. Asking students to repeat information that we've presented to them is a low-critical-thinking task. Spelling tests, traditional math problems, map tests, and recitations of historical dates and figures are all examples of DOK 1 tasks.

DOK 2 is skill/concept. This requires students to do some amount of figuring things out. That means not just asking them to do the same math problem with different numbers but something that genuinely differs from the example. Using a Jam to create a Venn diagram to compare and contrast two concepts can be a DOK 2 task.

> **TIP**
> Get in the habit of labeling student activities by DOK level to help progressively increase the DOK of tasks.

DOK 3 is strategic thinking. If a student is expected to be able to get an assignment right the first time without needing any feedback from the teacher, the task is unlikely to be DOK 3. Students might use Jamboard to gather research from a text into **Sticky Notes** in the Jam, arrange the common themes together, and visualize their thinking to help them prepare for writing a research paper that makes claims and supports them with evidence from the text.

"Live in DOK 2 and 3. Visit DOK 1 and 4."

—Shelley Burgess

DOK 4 is complex reasoning. While many DOK 4 tasks take place over extended time periods, time is not what defines a DOK 4 task. Instead, DOK 4 means that students have extended learning to a new context or drawn conclusions from multiple sources and media types. Jamboard allows students organize complex reasoning to help them find and make those connections.

It is easy to use Jamboard to replace paper for DOK 1 tasks, but Jams allow for students to demonstrate their learning at the DOK 2, 3, and 4 levels as well.

Sample Jam: DOK Jam Template

CREATIVE THINKING

"If you have 30 of the same thing, that is not a project, it is a recipe."
—Chris Lehmann

Creativity is not just arts and crafts. In the context of the 4 Cs, we ask students to think creatively. That means that they have enough flexibility in the directions to do something different from their neighbor. Jamboard breaks the mold of linear thinking and allows students to creatively express their ideas.

Mixing forms such as drawings, images, and digital tools allows students to more creatively express their work. Creative thinking does not come from filling out a graphic organizer or template. Allow students the opportunity to start with a blank canvas and creatively communicate their ideas.

Visible Learning

Dr. John Hattie has extensively read and cataloged educational research in order to rank practices by how effective they are for learning. Practices in schools should be modern and research based. Students who are doing the work, talking, thinking, and tracking tasks are more effective learners.

We encourage you to reference the work of Dr. Hattie for designing classroom experiences that maximize student learning when you're designing tasks for students using Jamboard.

visible-learning.org

Before You Begin

Google Jamboard is a core app in the Google Workspace bundle. Although it is free, the Google administrator for your school must turn the app on so that teachers and students can access and use it. Once the administrator turns it on, Jamboard will be accessible immediately through the app and the web.

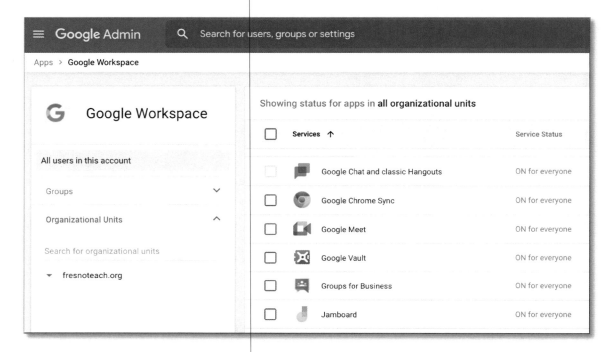

Sample Jams

For each of the teaching ideas in the book, we've provided you with at least one sample Jam. Use them to help guide you and your students toward greater proficiency with Jamboard, and make a copy of a Jam to use as the basis for your lessons. You can find all of the sample Jams at alicekeeler.com/jamboard.

> **TIP:** When creating templates, we recommend that you always keep the original intact. Create a folder in Drive called "Jamboard Templates" so that you can access them and/or redistribute copies to students if needed.

Jamboard Basics

1. Create a Jam

To start creating a Jam on the web version of Jamboard, use your browser to go to jamboard.google.com. To start with the mobile app, use the **Plus Icon** in the bottom right corner. You can also create a new Jam from Google Drive.

Once you've created a new Jam, it will be saved automatically, and you'll be able to find it in Drive. Click on "Recent" on the left side of the Google Drive page to find your new Jam, or return to jamboard.google.com to find all your Jams.

TIP

An easy way to create a new Jam right from your browser's address bar is to go to jam.new.

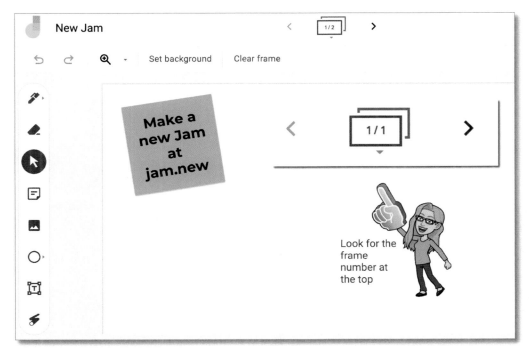

Make a new Jam at jam.new

Look for the frame number at the top

Sample Jam: New Jam

2. Share a Jam

Jamboard was not designed to replace paper but rather as a tool to better share ideas with others, so one of your first considerations when using it should be *who* you will be collaborating with.

Collaborate on a Jam by clicking on the **Share Button** in the upper right of the Jamboard page. This will open up the Google apps sharing dialogue box (just like you'd see in Google Docs, Sheets, or Slides). Invite someone to join you in whiteboarding by adding their email address here. Alternatively, you can choose to share with anyone in the domain or anyone with the link.

Share a Jam in Google Classroom by clicking the **Add Button** while creating an assignment and choose "Google Drive." Since Jam files live in Drive, you can add the Jam to an assignment in the same way you would add a Google Docs file. The default sharing setting in Google Classroom is "Students can view file," but Jams, unlike Docs, are designed to be interactive rather than only viewed. Change the sharing settings to "Students can edit file" or "Make a copy for each student."

> **TIP**
> To make sure a copy of a Jam is made when sharing it, change the end of the URL from "/edit" to "/copy."

In Google Contacts (contacts.google.com), create a label for groups of people you frequently share Jams with. If you label your students in a group, when you share a Jam, you can just type in the name of the group instead of each student's name.

Sample Jam:
Create a Contacts
Group to Share
a Jam

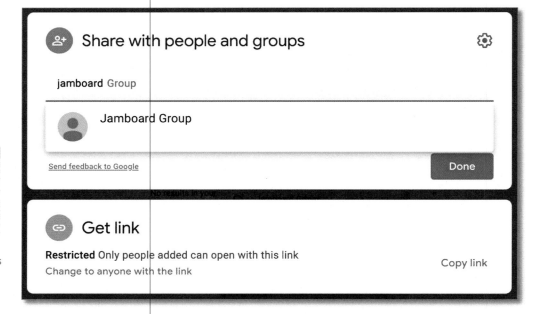

3. Rename a Jam

Once you create a Jam, you should rename the file immediately.

Sample Jam:
Rename a Jam

If you don't give a Jam a title, the file will be given the default name "Untitled Jam." While it's convenient that Jams automatically save to Drive, it can be hard to find the file you're looking for if there are many Jams with the default title, and using clear titles for documents helps students know what the assignment is and what they are working on.

In the upper left of Jamboard is the Jam title. Click on it to open a pop-up that allows you to rename the file. Alternatively, click on the **Three Dots Icon** "more actions" menu in the upper right and choose "Rename" from the menu.

Rename

> **TIP:** Numbering your assignments with a # and a three-digit number makes it easier for you and your students to get on the same page about which assignment you're referring to. Try adding the assignment number to Jam files (and other files) to make it clear what assignment the Jam is associated with. For example, you might name a Jam "#003 How Many Squares Activity."

4. Find a Jam

Jamboard Jams are just like files in Docs, Sheets, and Slides. Your Jams are all saved to Google Drive. Locate your Jams in Google Drive by searching at the top of Google Drive for "type:jam." This will filter your Drive for any Jams you have.

You can add a Jam to an assignment in Google Classroom by clicking on the **Add Button** and choosing Google Drive. In the **Drive Picker,** click on the **Three Lines Icon** to search for file type and choose "Jam."

TIP

Star a Jam in Drive so that it is easily accessible. Single click on the Jam in Drive and press "S" to star.

Q Search in Drive ⟶ ≡

▤ Text documents

▢ Presentations

✚ Spreadsheets

🖼 Images

🎞 Videos

▤ Forms

Jams

5. View the Version History

One of the best parts of using Google products is the ability to collaborate in real time or asynchronously on the same document. When collaborating, it can be very useful to see when (and by whom) changes to a document have been made. Jamboard automatically records new versions of Jams when they're edited by collaborators.

To see different versions of a Jam, access the version history by clicking on the **Three Dots Icon** or use the keyboard shortcut **Ctrl and Alt and Shift and H.**

Sample Jam:
Keyboard
Shortcuts Jam

TIP: You can reuse the same Jam templates year after year. After a class interacts with the Jam, restore it to its original version for the next school year.

6. Rescue a Lesson

While we wish all our lessons went perfectly, we know this is not the reality. Just as they do in any classroom, some unexpected student interactions can occur when using Jamboard. The **Clear Frame Button** in the top toolbar clears the entire frame and removes all **Sticky Notes** from it. A frame could be accidentally deleted during a session. Alice has been known to use a template (instead of a copy of a Jam) with her students and ruin it.

TIP

Use the **Three Dots Icon** on the version timestamp to "Make a Copy" to document evidence when parents or administrators need to be notified of a student's misbehavior.

Sample Jam:
Rescue a
Lesson Jam

When unexpected things happen while working with students, quickly get back to normal by using the **Three Dots Icon** in the top toolbar. Select "See version history." A sidebar on the right will reveal different edits on the Jam. Locate the last time you edited alone or before you made a change you want to undo. Clicking on the timestamp will allow you to rename the Jam to "Template." Click on "Restore this version" in the upper left.

7. Three Dots Icon for More Actions

Clicking on the **Three Dots Icon** at the top of Jamboard opens a menu that gives you options for more actions. Some of these actions include:

- Rename the Jam
- Make a copy of a Jam
- Downloading the Jam as a PDF file
- Remove a Jam
- Save a frame as an image

Sample Jam:
Three Dots Menu

Additionally, you can use the **Three Dots Icon** to get help from the community or leave the Jamboard team feedback.

Teach your students about the **Three Dots Icon** menu at the top of Jamboard

> **TIP:** Downloading the Jam as a PDF file will save all of the frames of the Jam. Have students create a Wakelet (wakelet.com) for the unit to organize what they have learned. Students can add the PDF of their Jam to the Wakelet.

8. Use the Frame Bar

A Jam is made up of multiple pages called frames.

At the top center of Jamboard is a rectangular **Frame Bar Icon** that indicates what frame you are on. The arrows to the left and right of the icon allow you to move back or forward a frame. Clicking on the tiny arrow underneath the **Frame Bar Icon** will expand the **Frame Bar** to let you see all the frames in a Jam and to quickly navigate to another frame.

While collaborating on a Jam, use the **Frame Bar** to see what frame a collaborator/student is on. A **User Icon** will appear above the frame thumbnail to show where another user is in the Jam.

Sample Jam:
Use the Frame Bar
Sorter Template

TIP

Check the **Frame Bar** to ensure that your students are with you on the correct frame.

9. Add a Frame

A new Jam has only one frame, but using multiple frames allows each of your students to share their thinking in their own space when collaborating on a single Jam.

To the right of the **Frame Bar Icon** is an arrow that allows you to navigate to the next frame. If there is not a next frame, clicking on the arrow will create a new frame.

Sample Jam:
Add a Frame
Template

You'll see a **Plus Icon** between the frames of the expanded **Frame Bar**. Clicking here allows you to insert a frame between two frames.

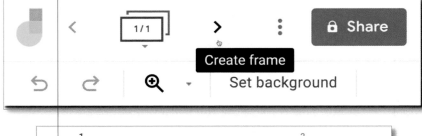

TIP

A Jam is limited to a maximum of twenty frames.

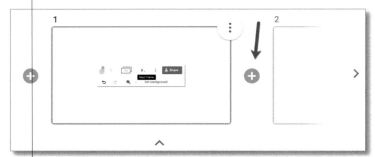

10. Delete a Frame

Not everything is meant to be permanent.

When you hover over a frame in the expanded **Frame Bar**, you will see a **Three Dots Icon** in the corner of each frame. Find the frame you want to delete, click on the **Three Dots Icon,** and select **Delete**. The frame will be permanently removed from the Jam.

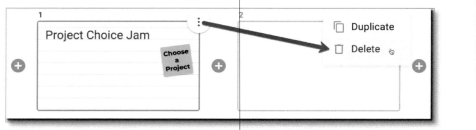

Sample Jam:
Project Choice
Template

TIP: Create a Jam for students with multiple project ideas on different frames. Students can choose a project and delete the frames that are not relevant to them.

11.   Reorganize Frames

When students are starting a project, whether they are collaborating with each other or just curating information, they may not realize that the information they're using needs to be in a specific order. Jamboard allows students to concentrate on the content goals of the assignment initially and then consider its sequence later.

Sample Jam: Rearrange the Frames Template

After expanding the **Frame Bar**, you can rearrange the frames in a Jam by dragging them.

> **TIP:** Create a Jam template where the frames are intentionally out of order. Have students use the **Frame Bar** to rearrange the frames and then explain each frame or complete a task on the frame.

12.   Duplicate a Frame

The best way to copy the contents of a frame is to duplicate the entire frame. This enables you to edit the content of the new frame rather than re-creating it from scratch.

When you hover over a frame in the expanded **Frame Bar**, you will see a **Three Dots Icon** in the corner of each frame. Find the frame you want to duplicate, click on the **Three Dots Icon,** and select **Duplicate**.

Sample Jam: Duplicate a Frame Template

There is a limit of twenty frames for a single Jam, but if you need more, just continue your work in a new Jam. Title the "continued" Jam accordingly, using titles like "New Jam Part 1" and New Jam Part 2."

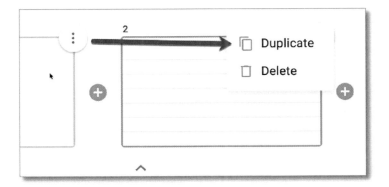

TIP

Duplicate a frame template before sharing with students to allow all students to be in the same document rather than creating individual documents for students.

13. Use the Pen Tool

A Jam frame is a blank canvas.

Having students use tools to visualize or work through a process graphically can aid their creative critical thinking. Jamboard provides users a way to do that by drawing freely on its canvas with the **Pen** tool, something that sets it apart from other Google Workspace apps.

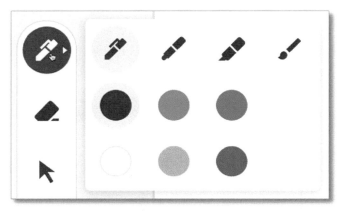

Find the **Pen** tool at the top of the side toolbar (on the left side of the screen). Clicking on it expands a menu of options, giving you access to a skinny pen, a thicker marker, a highlighter, and a brush.

Sample Jam:
Using the Pen Tool

Sample Jam:
Contrast for
Accessibility

TIP

Use a white or yellow pen on a **Sticky Note** with a dark background to create visual contrast and emphasize important information. This can also help reduce eye strain when reading content on the screen.

14. Create Sticky Notes

Sample Jam:
Using the Sticky
Note Tool

Sample Jam:
Sticky Note
Template

The **Sticky Note** tool is one of Jamboard's best features. It's a great way to share ideas that goes beyond the simple text box.

Locate the **Sticky Note Icon** in the middle of the side toolbar, or use the keyboard shortcut **Ctrl and Shift and P.**

Students can clearly show their interactions with an activity in Jamboard by using a **Sticky Note**. A great way to ask them to do this is to invite them to collaborate on a Jam by adding a **Sticky Note** to it with their idea about a topic.

TIP

Use different colors of **Sticky Notes** to categorize or sort information.

15. Adding an Image

Jamboard is a visual tool, so adding images enhances the communication of ideas. One of the most important capabilities of a Jam is the ability to drag and move things on the frame.

On the web version, use the **Add Image** tool in the side toolbar or paste an image using **Ctrl and V**. You can add images by dragging them to the **Image Uploader**. Use the **Camera** option to instead capture your webcam to add a picture to the frame.

Sample Jam:
Submit Your
Paperwork
Template

Avoid dragging the corners of the image when moving it, or else you might accidentally resize or distort the image.

TIP
Students can add pictures of work they've completed on paper to a Jam by using the **Camera** option in the **Uploader.**

16. Manage the Text Box

To add text to a frame, you will need to manually add text boxes by clicking on the **Text Box Icon** (which looks like a *T* with a box around it) in the side toolbar. Click anywhere on the frame to place the text box.

Use the resizing handles to change the dimensions of the box.

Text boxes have a style associated with them, which mainly indicates the size of the text in the box. The default style is "Normal." You can see (and change) the style for a box you have selected in the top toolbar.

> **TIP:** After creating a text box and resizing it, use the **Three Dots Icon** in the upper right of the text box to duplicate it. This way, you can create a set of boxes with consistent sizes.

Sample Jam: Managing the Text Box

17. Change the Background

Jamboard allows you to change the background of a frame. Built-in backgrounds include dots, lines, "graph paper" (blue or gray grids), and solid colors. You can also insert your own backgrounds, which can be used like templates for a frame.

To change the background of a frame, click on "Set background" in the top toolbar.

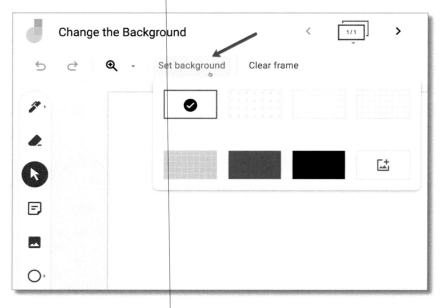

Jams are designed so that you can move things around within frames in order to organize and share ideas. When you insert your own background, it will be locked onto the frame, so students can move their ideas around without disturbing key elements of the template.

Sample Jam:
Change the
Background

Sample Jam:
Custom Lined
Paper Background
Jam

TIP

Upload your image into Google Slides, then download the slide as a JPEG file to prevent it from being distorted in Jamboard.

18.   Duplicate Objects

Add a picture or a **Sticky Note** to a Jam and use the **Three Dots Icon** on the upper-right-hand corner of the object to choose "Duplicate." Alternatively, the keyboard shortcut **Ctrl and D** will also duplicate an object.

In Jamboard, you can stack counters or pins for students to drag by duplicating images multiple times then piling the resulting copies directly on top of one another. Asking students to drag the objects in the frame—to organize, count, sort, vote, compare, or play with them—allows them to make connections between ideas and think through different ways of visualizing a concept.

Sample Jam:
Duplicate Objects
Template

Sample Jam:
Counting Bears

Sample Jam:
Map of the US

TIP

Be careful when adding objects and pen strokes to a Jam. If there are too many in a single Jam, there's a chance that the Jam might overload and crash.

19. Order Objects in the Frame

Jam frames have layers, so the order of objects in front of or behind the others is important. Initially, objects in a frame are layered in the order in which they are added. If you add a second image to a frame with one already on it, the second image will be on a layer in front of the first (and likewise for each object you add). But you can change the order of objects after you've added them.

> ### TIP
> Selecting "Bring to front" or "Send to back" from the "Order" menu allows you to hide objects or text behind an image.

Sample Jam:
Hide the Hint
Template

Sample Jam:
Behind the Circle

Click on the **Three Dots Icon** in the upper right of the object and select "Order" to send an object backward or forward in the layers of the frame.

20. Focus Collaboration with Laser Pointer

When collaborating on a Jam in real time, students will be viewing the Jam on their individual devices at the same time. A user—whether they're a student or a teacher—can use the **Laser Pointer** tool to bring attention to the work they're doing in a frame.

> ### TIP
> Ask students to use the **Laser Pointer** tool when they are contributing to a Jam and want to talk about their work.

Sample Jam:
Present Your Ideas
Template

The **Laser Pointer** tool can be found at the bottom of the side toolbar.

Even when students only have view access to the Jam, the Laser Pointer allows for real-time emphasis of elements in a Jam.

Jamboard can be a teaching tool that supports the 4 Cs of education—creativity, collaboration, critical thinking, communication—as well as two more: curation and computational thinking. All of the activities that follow use Jamboard to support one or more of these important skills.

21. Lose the Worksheets

An obvious use for Jamboard is to use it to replace paper worksheets, but it's important to remember that *digital is different*. Instead of just aiming to use Jamboard to replicate the function of a paper activity, it's important to keep in mind the advantages digital tools have. When designing activities with Jamboard, consider how students will interact digitally with the lesson—beyond just filling in answers.

Collaboration and creative thinking increase student engagement. Jamboard is designed with collaboration and idea-sharing at its core, and activities—including worksheets—should be designed with those strengths in mind.

What changes when instead of disseminating many copies of the same worksheet to your students, you share a *single* Jam with multiple students? Students will be more engaged when they share and collaborate on creative approaches to questions, rather than simply asking for the answers.

So, make a worksheet into a Jam and send it out to all of the students in a class, enabling them to respond by editing it. Then, together with the class, review the responses to the worksheet questions and engage students in a conversation about how they approached the questions.

If you are not using Google Classroom, click the **Share Button** to change the sharing permissions to "Anyone with the link can edit" or paste your student email addresses into the sharing field.

Students can view file ▼

If you are using Google Classroom, add the Jam to the assignment and change the sharing settings from "Students can view file" to "Students can edit file."

> **TIP:** Sometimes the right tool is *not* a Jam but rather a Google Form. Collecting student answers to questions in a form allows you to see all the responses in one place. Set the Form to automatically grade responses.

Sample Jam:
Collaboration
Norms

Sample Jam:
What Do You
Notice Template

Sample Jam:
Discuss the Main
Character

Sample Jam:
Coordinate Plane
Battleship

22. Compare Classes

Why clutter up your Google Drive when you can keep it clean with just one Jamboard Jam?

Try using the same Jam with multiple classes by creating a template and new versions for each class. Before sharing collaboratively with one class, use the **Three Dots Icon** in the upper right to "See version history." Click on the timestamp and create a version called "Template." After your first class completes the activity, click on the **Three Dots Icon** again to "See version history" and rename the current version with the time-stamp to reflect which class you used it with (e.g., "1st period").

Now, click on the version named "Template" and choose "Restore this version." Your Jam is ready to use with the next class. At the end of class, go back to the version history again to name the version after that class.

> **TIP**
>
> In the upper right of the version history is a toggle to "Only show named versions." This will make the version list easier to navigate if you have named versions for your classes.

Sample Jam:
Compare Classes
Template

Want to see how one class did compared to another? Review the version history and click on the named versions to easily see how different classes responded.

This will help you to prepare for the next day, to differentiate for each class, and to consider what additional focus you want to bring to your lesson.

23. Collaborate across Frames

Jamboard is a great way to keep students engaged in a lesson, and it allows the teacher to collaborate with whole classes in new and useful ways.

Sample Jam:
Show Your
Thinking

TIP
For larger classes, create a copy of the Jam and name the copy "Group 2." Divide the class in half and assign students to one of the two Jams.

Sharing a single Jam assignment with your class (instead of one copy per student) allows you to give feedback more quickly and efficiently. A great way to facilitate this is to have one frame for each student in the same Jam.

In a new Jam, create a frame template and use the **Frame Bar** to duplicate the frame for each of your students. Then, give all students edit access to the Jam.

Students can claim a frame by adding a **Sticky Note** with their name on it. You can easily jump to a frame that a student is working on by clicking on the **Collaborator Icon** in the upper-right-hand corner of Jamboard.

24. Thinking Together

Having many students work together in the same Jam isn't just an option that educators should allow for; it should be your driving principle when designing lessons.

So, upgrade tasks intended for one student working alone by redesigning them to be completed in a Jam by multiple students working together.

Design the template to provide prompts for the students to discuss and think through ideas, and create places in Jam templates for each student to add a **Sticky Note** with their name on it.

TIP
Each student can choose a color for the **Sticky Notes** they use consistently throughout the Jam to demonstrate their contributions to the activity.

Sample Jam:
Thinking Together

Sample Jam:
Pizza Angles

Sample Jam:
Circles Project
Planning

25. Help Students Take Ownership of Their Learning

When students are engaged, they take ownership of their learning. Students who seek out new ways to showcase their learning will often exceed your expectations. Jamboard provides students with a blank canvas to sketch out their thoughts and demonstrate what they have learned.

Often, teachers direct students about what medium to use ("make a Google Doc"), or we dictate an activity ("Make a poster") as part of an

Sample Jam:
Learning
Objective
Template

assignment when asking students to show us that they have learned a concept. Instead, consider leading with the learning objective rather than the medium or activity. The learning objective is not *the way* students will show they have learned, but rather *what* they will know or be able to do after the lesson.

Instead of defaulting to asking students to complete an assignment using Google Docs, provide them with choices, including the choice to use a Jam to show what they've learned.

> **TIP**
>
> Get students in the habit of creating a Jam to plan out the project or activity they will use to demonstrate their understanding of the learning objective.

26. Ask Students to Submit the Link to Their Frame

Sample Jam:
Submit the Link to
the Frame 1

In the web version of Jamboard, each frame in a Jam has a unique URL. This is important because it allows students to easily direct teachers to particular frames they might need feedback on, even if multiple students are working on the same Jam.

Students can copy URLs to frames directly from the address bar of their browser. When using Google Classroom, students should paste the link to their frame into the private comments, since they cannot submit links to collaborative documents they are not the owner of.

Sample Jam:
Submit the Link to
the Frame 2

Have students persevere in problem-solving by starting an activity in a Jam. They should work in stages, and each frame should build on information from the previous frame. The whole Jam will show all of their work, but at each phase of the project, students can submit links to the individual frame they've been working on.

> **TIP:** When reviewing student work, copy the link to the frame you are reviewing and paste it in the private comments of Google Classroom, or wherever you give feedback. This allows the student to quickly get back to the frame you are giving them suggestions on.

27. Have a Class Discussion

In Dr. John Hattie's research on maximizing student learning, one of the highest-ranked activities is class discussion. When the students are doing the talking, they are doing the learning.

In a traditional classroom setting, when the teacher asks a question, as soon as one hand goes up the thinking of other students goes down. Dr. Jo Boaler discourages the use of handraising to respond to a question since it promotes the idea that we value quick answers more than thoughtful ones. Using a digital tool like Jamboard allows all students to participate in a discussion, and it gives *all* students the time to think, not just those who can raise their hands first.

Sample Jam:
Classroom
Discussion
Template

Here's a great way to create Jams to facilitate class discussion:

Start by creating a Jam with a single frame—when you make the Jam live, you want all of your students on the same frame. Then, post a discussion question onto the frame using a text box and the "Title" style. Share the Jam with your students in real time and ask them to create **Sticky Notes** in the frame with their *initial* responses to the prompt. The Jam is not the whole discussion but rather a starter for it. Students can use the ideas of all their peers to guide the in-class verbal discussion.

Sample Jam:
Microscope
Discussion

TIP

Move and group the **Sticky Notes** in a discussion. Common themes or ideas can be dragged and grouped together.

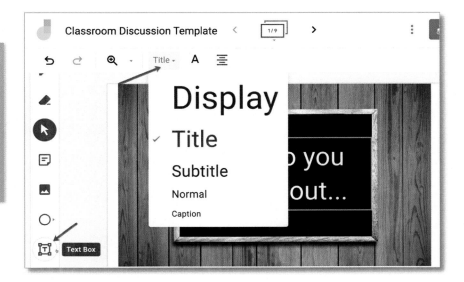

28. Use Graph Paper

Graph paper encourages students to design, and it is useful for all subject areas and grade levels.

Sample Jam:
Use Graph Paper

Jamboard has built-in "graph paper" backgrounds. Using it for Jams, can help set students up to design work that utilizes their learning objectives.

To use the graph paper background in a frame, click on "Set background" in the top toolbar, and choose "Blue graph" or "Gray graph." (A new frame created within the Jam will default to the blank background, and you'll have to change it, or you can copy a frame with a background already on it.)

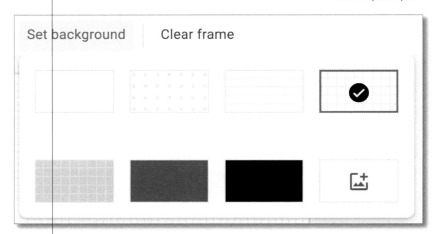

> **TIP:** Jamboard is designed for collaboration around ideas. Regularly encourage students to work together by designing ideas together in a Jam.

29. Create a Graphic Organizer

Graphic organizers give students templates for organizing their thinking, and they are an essential part of any classroom.

Jams allow you to set a custom background that can work as a graphic organizer. This background is locked down to allow students to use the graphic organizer without moving it.

Click on "Set background" in the top toolbar and select the last option to add an image.

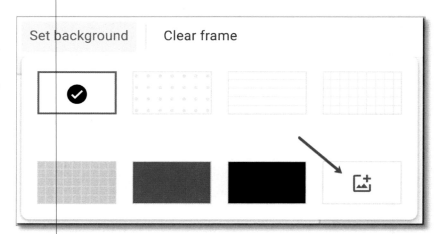

Design your graphic organizer in Google Slides. Slides have the same dimensions as Jams, making it easy to ensure that your graphic organizer uploads without distortion.

Use the **File menu** in Google Slides, choose "Download," and select the JPEG format. In Google Chrome, the downloaded Google Slides image will show in the download bar at the bottom of the browser. Drag the image file from the download bar into **Uploader** for "Set background" in your Jam.

Sample Jam:
Google Drawing
9600 by 5400
Jam Background
Template

TIP

If your graphic organizer looks pixelated, create it at a higher resolution in a tool such as Google Drawing. Try 9600 X 5400 pixels in Google Drawing.

30. Create a Do Now Jam for the Week

Activities to get students started in the first minutes of class go by many names, but Jamboard is a great tool to use for any of them, whether they're open-ended questions, writing prompts, reflections on the previous day's learning, or anything else.

To create a Do Now Jam that prompts students to complete a task when class has begun, create one frame for each day of the week. Add the directions and expectations on the first frame, then, on each additional frame, add the date and a prompt for the students to complete. Each day, the students will fill in one frame with their responses.

Google Classroom users can add the Jam to an assignment by clicking on "Add" and choosing "Google Drive." Change the file permissions to "Make a copy for each student."

Sample Jam:
Do Now Jam

Because of Jamboard's built-in collaborative features, you do not have to collect the activity each day to review student responses and leave feedback. You and the student have access to the Jam at the same time.

> **TIP**
>
> Reduce the amount of record keeping you need to do by creating one Jam document for the week rather than daily recording student participation for each day.

31. Create a Choice Board

Choice is powerful. It gives students motivation and a locus of control. Even if the choices are as simple as "answer question A or answer question B," students feel empowered by being able to make a decision.

> **TIP**
>
> Students with low self-efficacy will choose to do nothing rather than feel dumb. Consider adding a choice that any student can feel successful at.

Additionally, when you provide choice to students, you are differentiating and meeting students at different levels. Choice provides students the opportunity to own their learning and to feel successful at the same time.

Give students options on the first frame of a Jam using **Sticky Notes** that they can drag to a selection area. Students then complete their work in additional frames.

Sample Jam:
Choice Board
Template

32. Peer Feedback

Giving feedback is a skill that must be taught. Use Jamboard to have students give peer feedback in real time. You can review the feedback students are giving for accuracy and facilitate a conversation around it.

Sample Jam:
Peer Feedback
Sample

Take a screenshot of selected student work samples or download samples from Google Slides. Add the student work samples to the background of Jam frames. This locks down the student work onto the background. Share the Jam with your students and ask them to add **Sticky Notes** with their feedback.

> **TIP**
>
> Have students color code their feedback: green to indicate something done well, orange for suggestions for improvement, and pink for errors or inaccuracies.

33. Concept Mapping and Charts

Jamboard is a great tool to target visual learners. Students can create flow charts, concept maps, diagrams, and illustrations. They can categorize information to chart their knowledge or plan out their logic. It's a great way to check in visually with students and get a sense of where they are with their understanding of a concept. Jamboard also gives you the opportunity to provide feedback and conference with students to allow them to explain their thought processes.

Students can use the **Shape** tool to create a concept map, flowchart of how to solve a problem, or a Venn diagram on the similarities and differences of concepts.

Sample Jam: STEM Flowchart

Sample Jam: Concept Map Templates

Sample Jam: Using the Shape Tool

Sample Jam: Digitize the Writing Process

Sample Jam: Windows Snaps Creativity by Brigid Duncan

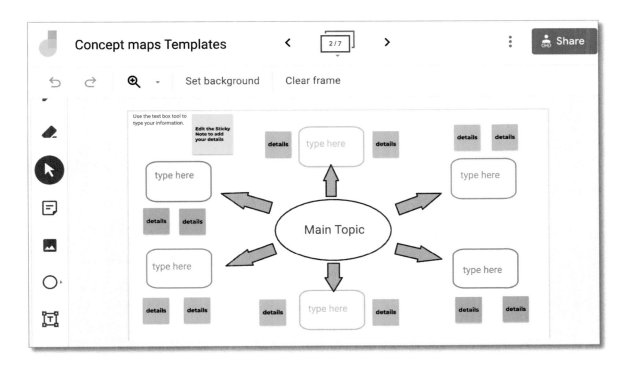

34. Explore Concepts

Before giving students information, consider the lesson-plan model called "the 5 Es": engage, explore, explain, extend, evaluate. Notice that "explain" comes third!

Engage students in a concept by creating a collaborative Jam to have them work together to discuss a topic, look for patterns, and draw conclusions. Even if the students do not figure out the procedures, they will realize that they need the teacher to explain them.

> "It is not our job to rescue the students from thinking."
>
> —Dr. Jo Boaler.

TIP

Start a lesson with students already thinking. Ask them to collaborate on exploring an idea and communicate their results.

Have students work together in groups in a Jam to explore a concept, then have each group share their conclusions. After you've learned what needs to be explained further, transition to your lesson.

Sample Jam:
Genetics—Punnett Square

Sample Jam:
Graphing Sine and Cosine
by Diana Herrington

35. Context Clues

Sample Jam:
Mystery Meet
Template

When it comes to vocabulary, rather than explicitly telling students a word's definition, you can create a higher-DOK-level task by having students use context clues to figure out its meaning.

Create a Jam and ask students to add **Sticky Notes** with what they think something means based on the context provided. Students working together in a Jam can debate by citing evidence from the text.

A popular teaching activity is to connect with another classroom (in another state, or even country), using a video conferencing tool such as Google Meet, to have one class guess where the other class is located. The mystery class can only answer yes or no questions from your classroom, such as "Are you located near water?"

Sample Jam:
English Definitions

TIP: Jams are the perfect platform for students to strategically figure things out. They can cross off or add notes on their thoughts as they narrow in on a solution.

Have a map of the US or the world in a Jam for your class to mark off locations to help them narrow in on where in the world the mystery class is from.

36. Feedback Frames

Add a new frame to student Jams to give yourself space to provide feedback within the Jam. Copy the link to your feedback frame into the private comments of Google Classroom, or wherever you leave comments for students on their work.

When leaving comments to students on their work in a Jam, paste the link for the student to the frame you are referencing. This helps the student to quickly make updates and provide context to your feedback comment.

Sample Jam:
Feedback
Frames
Template

TIP

When reviewing student work, create a Jam with different feedback on different frames. That way, you can send multiple students links to frames they need to see, but all students will have access to all of the feedback frames to review.

37. Teaching Critical Thinking

Thinking is messy and should require strategizing and multiple attempts. A student's first attempt at something will usually not be correct if it requires advanced critical thinking. Ask students to include their strategy on a Jam so you can see their "failed" attempts before they came to a final conclusion.

Students can use the **Frame Bar** in Jamboard to duplicate the frame. After making an initial attempt at an assignment, they should not erase their work but rather duplicate the frame to show the journey of their thinking process.

TIP

Start with the problem/ challenge and then have the students use a Jam to brainstorm what essential questions they need to answer in order to address the challenge.

Jam's built-in **Sticky Notes** allow students to put down a lot of ideas and drag them around to determine which ones go together, which will contribute to the solution, and which ones do not make the final cut.

Critical thinking is not accomplished by following steps and directions. Provide constraints that make it challenging to answer a prompt.

Sample Jam:
Share Your
Strategy Template

Sample Jam:
Open Middle
Template

Sample Jam:
Free Choice
Shopping Spree
Activity

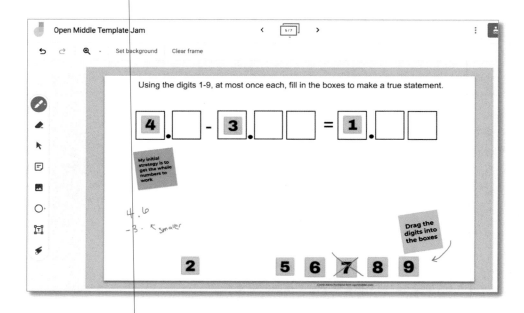

38. Make Inferences

Jamboard helps students to demonstrate critical thinking skills they use when making inferences from provided materials. Ask students to make observations and draw conclusions based on evidence in a text or image that you've provided. Have them add **Sticky Notes** with their comments. Afterward, you can lead a discussion about their findings.

Design a background image template in Google Slides with an image that leaves room to the sides of the image for student inferences. Change the background of the frame to the image you want to focus on to prompt a discussion with your students.

Sample Jam:
Images and
Inferences

Sample Jam:
Image Usage
Type

TIP
Using photosforclass.com will automatically add an attribution to the bottom of an image.

39. Sorting

Jamboard is great for helping students think through ideas because it allows you to easily move and organize information. Students can use a Jam to sort by order, arrange data, and sequence events.

When creating critical thinking activities, consider the need for productive struggle in student thinking. Jams allow students to easily make initial attempts at work and to think through whether something should be done differently.

Provide students with sorting challenges that require DOK 2–level skills, which involve trying to figure out how a task can be accomplished.

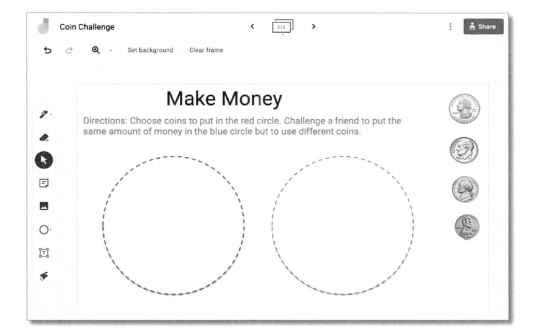

Sample Jam:
Coin Sorting
Challenge

Sample Jam:
Money Jam

Sample Jam:
Cite Evidence
from the Text

TIP: Use Alice's add-on for Google Docs by going to alicekeeler.com/doctoslides. This allows you to send text from a Google Doc to an individual slide in Google Slides. Download the slide as an image and add it to a Jam to make it easy to drag around on a frame.

Sample Jam:
A to Z Template

40. Keep the Lesson Going

Sharing learning objectives or daily agendas in a Jam has advantages over writing them on a traditional whiteboard: Students can access the Jam on their individual device—be they in person or remote. They can be prompted to check in with a **Sticky Note** on the Jam, participate in a warm-up activity, or contribute their ideas to the day's classroom discussion. Rather than being static and prewritten, lessons in a Jam can dynamically evolve during the class, or even into future classes.

Sample Jam:
Daily Objectives–
Hurricane Project

Sample Jam:
Nonrenewable
and Renewable
Merge Cube

TIP

Keep a Jam on hand for each day's lesson and share it with the students. Build and add to the notes as the lesson progresses. Students can have access to these notes after the lesson and at home.

41. Change Your Lesson

When a student asks you a question, it can very often take your lesson in a different direction, as it should. Using a Jam with students allows you to gather data from them in real time and make adjustments to your lessons on the fly.

That's more challenging with a presentation tool like Google Slides where you are locked into the slide order after you've begun a presentation. But Jamboard is interactive, and additional frames can be added at any time. When something new comes up, all you have to do is say, "That is an interesting question, let's add a frame and everyone add a Sticky Note with . . ."

TIP: Student-centered lessons involve the students doing the talking. In his book *Visible Learning*, Dr. Hattie shows that the teacher does over 80 percent of the talking in a typical lesson. Choose Jamboard to increase student interactivity and give students more voice.

Sample Jam:
KWL Template

42. Compare and Contrast

Comparing and contrasting can be a DOK 2–level activity.

Use a Jam to give students an opportunity to think through how two events or concepts are similar and different. Each similarity or difference would be added to its own **Sticky Note** using a different color for each concept. This allows students to easily sort and group the concepts and clearly identify the contrasts.

Sample Jam:
Venn Diagram
Template

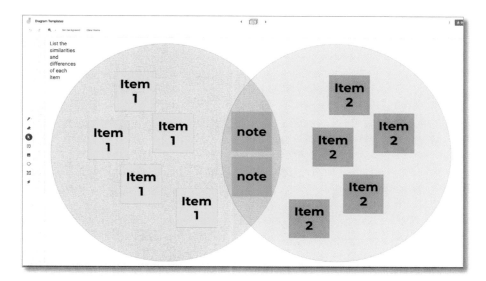

Sample Jam:
Cause and Effect
Bonefish Template

> **TIP:** Pair students up to work together on a single Jam. Each student should add **Sticky Notes** to their own frame with what they know about a concept. The students would then compare and contrast what they came up with independently.

Sample Jam:
Analyzing
and Finding
Conclusion

43. Organize Students

When organizing student seating or groups, there are many factors to consider. Jamboard is the perfect tool to sort and organize groups of students.

Using Google Slides, create an image with circles or boxes to represent each group, then download the slide as an image and add it to the background of a Jam frame. Add each student's name to the Jam on **Sticky Notes**.

You can duplicate the frame multiple times to try different arrangements before making a final decision.

TIP

Create a QR code for your seating chart to allow a substitute teacher to know how your students are arranged.

You can also put student names on **Sticky Notes** or insert their school photo into a frame to help create a schedule.

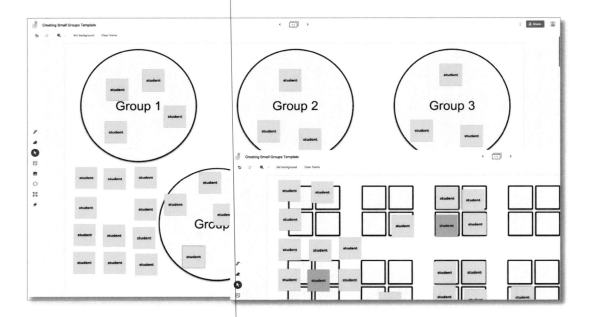

Sample Jam:
Seating Chart

Sample Jam:
Small Groups

Sample Jam:
Station Cards

Sample Jam: Make
Appointment
Template

Sample Jam:
Today's Schedule

44. Sketchnoting with Jamboard

Sketchnoting is a way to take notes graphically, and it's a great way for students to comprehend and retain information. The ideas are not captured in complete sentences, and Sketchnotes often use no words at all. It's a great method to help students interpret, record, analyze, and organize information. Plus, it supports creativity and expression. Unlike regular notes that go linearly down the page, Sketchnotes can tell the story of a lesson anywhere, and they're perfect for the frame of a Jam.

Students can use the **Pen** tool to create drawings that represent their notes, and **Sticky Notes** can be added to function as labels. Students can use the **Add Image** tool to search for icons or pictures from the web to add to their Sketchnote.

Sketchnoting is a creative critical-thinking activity: students need to identify the key information that builds the story of the lesson and make a decision about how to represent it visually. This is a skill that must be taught. Simply asking students to draw their notes is insufficient. Get students started with Sketchnotes by asking them to watch a YouTube video of a dynamic speaker, perhaps a TED talk, and take notes during the video. Create and share a Jam with the class to brainstorm what they got out of the talk and how they would visualize it before collectively creating a Sketchnote.

Sample Jam: Sketchnoting with Jamboard Sample

Sample Jam: Sketchnote Notetaking by Brigid Duncan

Sample Jam: Sketch the Lesson

TIP

Practiced Sketchnoters can create their Sketchnote while participating in a presentation. Beginners will need time to create their Sketchnote from their notes after the presentation.

45. Create a Back-Channel

TIP

Use the Tab Resize Chrome extension to manage your back-channel and other content while you are teaching.

Consider creating a back-channel for students to discuss or share ideas during a presentation without disturbing the presenter.

Create and share a Jam, giving your students editing rights. Explain to students that they will be using a Jam to back-channel during (synchronously) the lesson to respond to each other during a session.

Sample Jam: Back-Channeling Template

46. Parking Lot

Parking Lots provide a place for off-topic ideas or follow-up, but unlike back-channels, Parking Lots are typically asynchronous.

Traditionally, Parking Lots are created on large poster paper and hung up in the classroom. Students write their ideas on a paper sticky note—especially feedback or anything that they want to follow up on later—and "park" it on the poster paper.

Obvious challenges with a paper Parking Lot include participants not being able to access the poster easily to place notes, notes falling off or getting lost, and students having difficulty seeing what's posted (sometimes, the notes must be read aloud). Saving the paper Parking Lot is a challenge as well, especially because they can take up a lot of valuable storage space once they're taken off the wall.

All these problems are solved with a Jamboard Parking Lot.

Design a graphic organizer for students to add **Sticky Notes** to. Common categories include:

- Questions
- Follow-up
- Ideas
- Need help
- Opportunities
- Get rid of
- What is working
- What is not working
- Ideas for change

Sample Jam:
Parking Lot
Template

TIP

Use the **Ctrl and X** keyboard shortcut to cut a **Sticky Note** from a "to-do" frame, and use **Ctrl and V** to paste it into an "in-progress" or "complete" frame to show that action has been taken on the idea.

47. Access a Document

You can use Jamboard to host conversations around external documents and include the Google Doc, Slides, or PDF document right in the Jam.

This feature is only available in the mobile app or the Kiosk, but once something has been added to the Jam you can switch to using the web version.

Click the **Plus Icon** on the side toolbar in the Jam to "Insert" and choose "Drive content." This will allow you to insert placeholder images of the pages of your file. Expand the file images to drag a particular page out as an image onto the frame.

Jams only allow you to take a snapshot in time of a document and add one page at a time to the Jam. Any updates to the document

Sample Jam:
Add a Document
to a Jam

you make after importing it will not appear in the Jam. This can be a feature—it aids in documenting and developing the process of ideation by showing what a project looked like in an early stage and what conversations and ideas the team had around how to shape it.

Holly Clark, teacher and author of *The Google Infused Classroom*, recommends adding reading passages into a Jam. Students can cite evidence from the text by highlighting it right in the Jam and adding **Sticky Notes** that make connections and elaborate on ideas.

TIP
Instead of adding screenshots of documents to an image, add the pages right onto a Jam frame.

48. Track Accomplishments

Students of all ages love to receive stickers and badges, so why not provide them digitally? Creating a visual record of students' accomplishments or mastery of standards by distributing digital badges can help promote engagement and provide students with motivation to complete a task. It is a great way to communicate progress and celebrate success with students.

You can create your own badges using something like Google Drawings, Google Slides, or Canva. Download badges as PNG files, which allow for transparent backgrounds.

To present the badges to your students, you can create a new Jam for each individual or a Jam with a frame for each student. Add each badge to the Jam or add them to a Google Drawing or Slide to create a grid of badges you can use as the background of a Jam. In the Jam, use a white square to cover each badge. As students earn a badge simply delete the square covering it.

Create a grid of badges

> **TIP:** Use alicekeeler.com/badgegrid for a Google Slides add-on that generates circles to use when making badges.

Sample Jam:
Digital Badges

Sample: Google
Drawings
Badge Grid

Sample: Google
Drawings Blank
Badge Grid

Sample Jam:
Badge Reveal

49. Play Games

Jamboard makes an excellent platform for creating games that students can play collaboratively. Games can be used just for fun during a rainy day recess, but they can also work as a hook or a shared experience that leads into a lesson or discussion.

Use Jamboard to recreate the games you love or allow students to create their own games. Be sure students define the objective and rules of the game. You can also give them the opportunity to design the game pieces. Then, watch the magic happen.

Sample Jam:
Design a
Game Board

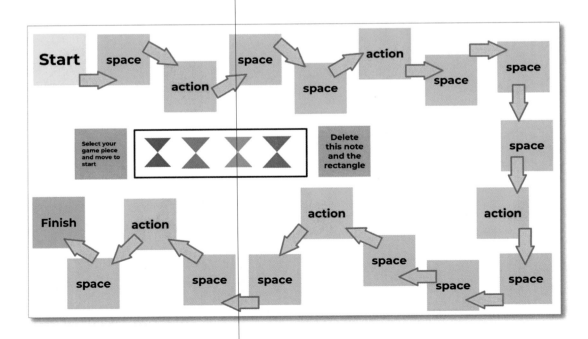

You can design a game board in Google Drawings or Google Slides, download it, and set it as the background in your Jam frame. **Add images** to the Jam for game pieces that can be dragged and placed around the board.

> **TIP:** Justin Coffey turns regular board games, such as Connect Four, into review games. Students get to play their turn if they answer a question correctly. An incorrect answer means they forfeit their turn.

Sample Jam:
Jamboard
Game Pieces

Sample Jam:
Master Mind
Game Template

Sample Jam:
Christmas
Memory Game
by Brigid Duncan

Sample Jam:
Connect Four

50. Gamification

Gamification helps to make activities more fun and thus more engaging by turning learning activities into games. Engagement matters! When students are engaged in an activity, they learn more.

Jamboard can help you gamify activities by allowing you to theme the activity and create draggable game pieces.

Gamify an activity by adding game elements like:

- competition
- storylines
- "levels"
- achievements and badges

Sample Jam:
Bingo in Jamboard

Sample Jam:
I Spy

Sample Jam:
Jeopardy

> **TIP**
> Provide immediate feedback by hiding answers or clues under boxes or images.

51. Have Students Create Puzzles

Puzzles require strategic thinking, and Jams are excellent tools to help students think through ideas and figure out challenges, helping them think outside of the box and be creative and innovative at the same time.

> **TIP**
>
> Use a dark background and a contrasting ink color to prevent eye strain.

Have students create a crossword puzzle in Jamboard to demonstrate how well they understand a concept. Students can design a board and create the clues (and answers) right in a Jamboard frame. They can even differentiate the puzzles by creating more or less complex puzzle designs and harder or easier clues.

There are many other kinds of puzzles that students can create in Jamboard.

Sample Sheet: Logic Puzzle Template

Sample Jam: Vacation Scheduling Logic Puzzle

Sample Jam: Which Lines are Parallel

Sample Jam: Crossword Puzzle Template

Spreadsheet Crossword Puzzle Template

52. Mystery Spot

A Mystery Spot activity is a great way to make working with ideas exciting and engaging, and it's easy to make in Jamboard. Use it to make a text box, image, or **Sticky Note** vanish in thin air.

> **TIP:** Initially, change your background to a dark background to help you ensure you have covered all of the space for your mystery spot with the **Pen** tool, when you're done, you can change the background back to white.

Use the **Pen** tool and select the marker to scribble with a white pen in an area on the frame about the size of your text, image, or **Sticky Note**. Pen strokes do not move and are always layered on top of other items in a frame. If you scribble enough with the marker, you can create a "white-out" that is invisible when you use a white background. When you drag images, text boxes, or **Sticky Notes** into the mystery spot, they will disappear.

Sample Jam: Pull a Rabbit Out of the Hat

Sample Jam: Mystery Jam

Sample Jam: Piggy Bank Mystery Spot

Sample Slides: Make a Mystery Spot Jam

53. Make Scratchers

Choice empowers students, and gamification increases engagement, so why not combine the two in a mystery choice Jam?

Sample Jam: Scratchers Template

> **TIP**
>
> Save and reuse the template to ensure that your scratchers are always in the same spot.

Create a frame with a background using images that represent different choices. Use the **Pen** tool to scribble over the choice images with a solid color until the images are hidden. When the students make their choice, they can use the **Eraser** tool to scratch off the **Drawing strokes** and reveal what's beneath.

The mystery you hide might be a variety of constraints for an activity or project.

Sample: Google Slides Scratchers Template

54. Reflections

Reflections are an essential part of the learning process that help students understand *how* they've learned.

Share a single Jam with the class and ask them to reflect back on the lesson. Ask them "What did you learn? What did you do well at? What did you fail at? What do you need to change?" They can write their answers in sticky notes and collaborate by grouping similar responses together in a frame.

> **TIP**
>
> Allow students to give feedback anonymously so that no one feels targeted when posting their reflections.

You can also ask students to reflect using rubrics. Create a rubric and upload it as the background to a Jam frame. This is particularly useful when having students work in small groups. Have the students in the group discuss how well they did on various criteria, including how well the group worked together, contributed, or focused on a particular task. This will provide you, as the teacher, with helpful information on forming small groups and who are the leaders in a group.

In fact, while these reflections provide students an opportunity to think about the lesson and increase their learning, they also give you valuable information on how to adjust the lesson the next day, helping you consider whether your students got out of the lesson what you anticipated. Students can give you a fresh

Sample Jam: Exit Ticket Template

Sample Jam: STEM Missions Reflections

Sample Jam: Lesson Reflection Template

Sample Jam: Rubric Reflections

perspective on the lesson, activity, or learning goal. This feedback is valuable, especially if a lesson proved to be boring or not very engaging. Use Jamboard as a platform for students to post comments or questions about what worked, what failed, and what needs improvement so that you can adjust the lesson accordingly for the next class.

55. Map the Story

Good teaching is storytelling, whether you're teaching math, English, history, or any other subject. The elements of a story (exposition, conflict, climax, resolution, etc.) are present in everyday situations. In fact, we often make sense of the seeming randomness of our day by relaying it in story form when someone asks how our day was. We provide context (exposition), describe what we wanted and what the obstacles were (conflict), how we achieved or failed to meet our objectives (climax), and what we learned or what the impact of our success or failure was (resolution).

TIP

Provide sentence stems in the Jam for students to respond to after the lesson.

Sample Jam:
Map the Lesson
Template

Copying notes word for word is DOK 0, but student engagement and learning increases when students go beyond copying and use their notes to tell stories.

Have students use a Jam to map out the story from the lesson. What did they learn? What connections can they make? Students can work in small groups on a single Jam to talk about the story of the lesson and to map out what they learned and how it fits together.

Teaching Content with Jamboard

Being intentional in choosing the right tool for an activity is key to the success of a lesson. Sometimes technology like Jamboard is right, and sometimes regular paper is. Just because you *can* do something in Jamboard does not necessarily mean that you *should*.

Rather than trying to squeeze a square peg into a round hole just for the sake of using Jamboard, always consider what medium and tool will actually work best for student learning and engagement. Do you want to create a collaborative creative experience? Then Jamboard might be the right tool for the job.

56. Dragging and Labeling

Simply labeling a diagram is a low-critical-thinking activity. Before using a Jam for a labeling activity, consider using tools, such as Quizlet Diagrams, that provide students with immediate feedback.

Always be critical about your choices of tools for an activity. Is your time best spent reviewing what students wrote or dragged into a box on a Jam?

Jams allow you and your students to have awesome collaborative experiences. However, Jamboard is not always the right tool.

Jams provide the best experience across Google apps when it comes to dragging things. Google Slides is certainly collaborative and can be interactive when used in edit mode, but moving things on a slide can be awkward. Each object on a Google Slide is actually a text box, so you can accidentally modify text when trying to move an object. It is also easy to accidentally resize an item on a Google Slide. Jamboard is designed for moving ideas around. It's smooth and almost effortless to add a **Sticky Note** or a text box to a Jam and move it.

Science Learning Hub: Label the Microscope

Jamboard offers students the ability to label diagrams or create their own interpretation of a concept. This gives students the opportunity to document their learning and explain it in their own words.

Create a Jam with your students and ask them to drag **Sticky Notes** to label a concept or think through the flow of the steps of a process.

Increase the DOK level by creating more labels than necessary and asking students to decide which of them they need. Have students delete the extra labels.

TIP

Change the order of images so that the one students need is on the bottom of other objects. Simply click on the image, then the **Three Dots Icon,** and select "Order," then "Send to back."

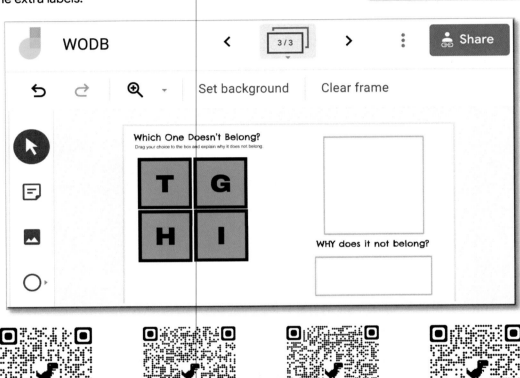

Sample Jam:
Draw and Label
an Animal Cell

Sample Jam:
Which One
Doesn't Belong

Sample Jam:
CH Sounds

Sample Jam:
Window Shopping
Activity

Sample Jam:
1st Grade
Sight Words

Sample Jam:
Geometry Proofs

Sample Jam:
Pull a Rabbit Out
of the Hat

57. Share What You Know

Jamboard allows the students to be the experts in the room by giving each student a voice to contribute to the lesson.

Help them share by creating a Jam template with text boxes listing different topics (use the "Title" style), and asking them to add a **Sticky Note** with something they know about the topic. Students can add the notes directly themselves or one person can record the facts shared during a lesson by adding a **Sticky Note** to the Jam.

Sample Jam: Share What You Know by Scott Marsden

58. What Is Going On in This Graph?

Data analysis and visualization can be done in any subject area in any classroom. In the age of big data, it is essential for all students to be data literate, especially when modern data visualizations are often more complex than a pie chart or bar graph.

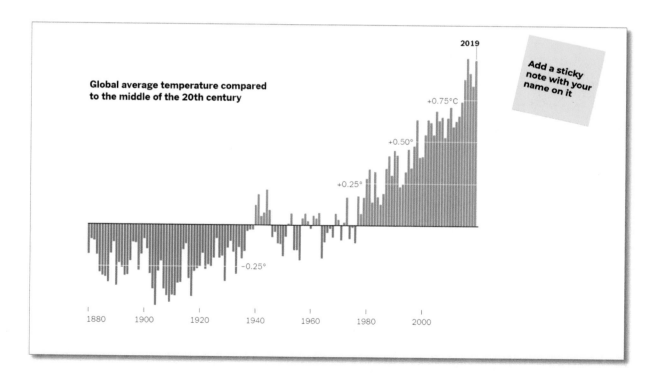

Sample Jam:
Analyze the Graph

Sample Jam:
What Is Going On
in This Graph

Sample Jam:
Analyze a Graph
Template

Get students in the habit of looking at a variety of ways that data can be displayed. What do they notice? What patterns can they identify? Find data visualizations outside of textbooks, like complex charts or infographics from the news, and add them to the first frame of a Jam, where your students can post **Sticky Notes** with their initial observations. Add the same visualization to the second frame and ask, "What other observations do you have?" Use as many frames as necessary to keep pushing students to make more and deeper observations.

Alternatively, give the students their own copy of the Jam. Duplicate the chart on different frames with each frame having additional sentence stems to keep pushing them to think deeper about the graph.

The key to teaching kids how to be critical analyzers is to avoid doing the thinking for them. Show them a graph and ask them what they see. No matter what they answer, try not to let your facial expression give away what you think about what they said. Ask, "OK, now what else?" Then ask, "Why do you think that is?" And keep pushing, asking questions like, "What do you think that means?"

> **TIP:** The *New York Times* puts out a weekly resource to get kids analyzing graphs from the newspaper: nytimes.com/column/whats-going-on-in-this-graph.

59. Research and Brainstorming

Students can use Jamboard to curate information about a topic. Jams are a great place to sort through information and make decisions.

Students can document the information using the **Pen** tool or **Sticky Note** tool, or they can add images that support their research. The critical thinking part of a research project is not the recording of facts but rather making decisions about what facts to use, how they connect together, and how to communicate them.

TIP

Create a Jam with the research requirements on different frames to help students with the research process.

Sample Jam:
Research
Template

Sample Jam: Student
Sample—World War II
by Gavin Mattina

Sample Jam:
Fish Ecosystem
Activity Sample

Using a Jam helps students researching a group project bring their ideas together, synthesize ideas from multiple sources, and work through a final presentation.

60. Show Different Approaches

Apps like PhotoMath and websites such as mathway.com will show students step-by-step solutions to math problems.

Using Jamboard, teachers can show that they value creative approaches to solving problems. Jamboard allows for changing the question from "What is the answer?" to "What are two ways to solve this?" Showing multiple ways to approach a prompt or problem requires the student to understand the concept beyond simply memorizing a set of procedures.

TIP

Have students use an app or website to find the solution to a problem, then screenshot it and add it to a Jam. Students can then contrast different ways to approach the same problem.

What are 2 ways to make: **$0.75**

Remove money from each jar so they each have $0.75

Sample Jam: Let's Two-Step

Sample Jam: What Is Your Strategy?

Sample Jam: Money Jam— Represent Multiple Ways

Sample Jam: Multiple Circles

Sample Jam: Solve It Another Way

61. Use Youcubed Activities

Youcubed is a nonprofit organization out of Stanford University that aims to reframe students' mathematical mindsets. The website youcubed.org has many math tasks that highlight how creative and visual math can be that can be downloaded and used in class. Adding Youcubed tasks to Google Jamboard allows students to creatively visualize their mathematical reasoning.

Start with the Week of Inspirational Math on the youcubed.org website. Locate the activity of your choice and use the "Download as PDF" option. This allows you to print the activity and distribute it to students.

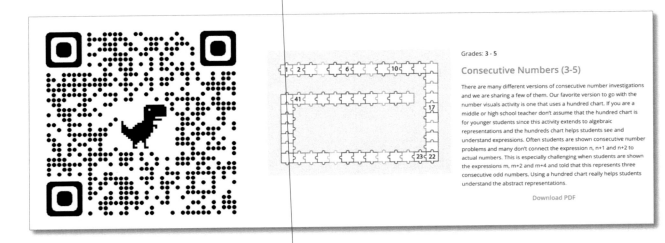

Use a screenshot tool to capture graphics. Add the screenshots to a Google Slides deck and download it as a JPEG image to add as the background. You can also add the screenshots to a Jam using the **Add Image** tool to create manipulatives.

TIP: Click on the Omnibox address bar in Google Chrome to automatically create a QR code (like one linking to Youcubed videos or directions). Download the QR code and add it as an image to a Jam to link students to additional information to help them with the activity.

Sample Jam:
Rod Trains
by Youcubed

Sample Jam:
Consecutive
Integers by
Youcubed

Sample Jam:
Exploring Calculus

62. Create Manipulatives

Visualizing concepts helps students to better understand what they are learning. The ability to create manipulatives, visualization tools that students can move around, is one way that Jamboard can help students better understand a concept.

Google Slides is often suggested as the go-to tool for math manipulatives. However, when moving objects in Google Slides, it's too easy to accidentally resize them, making for a frustrating experience. The open canvas of a Jam can be a more comfortable space to allow students opportunities to interact with math manipulatives.

TIP

You can insert the degree symbol by holding down the ALT key and typing the numbers 0176. For more information on typing special characters, google "ASCII alt codes."

Create manipulatives in a Google Drawing to take advantage of that platform's default transparent background and make sure to download images as PNG files to preserve the transparency before importing the image into Jamboard with the **Add Image** tool in the top toolbar.

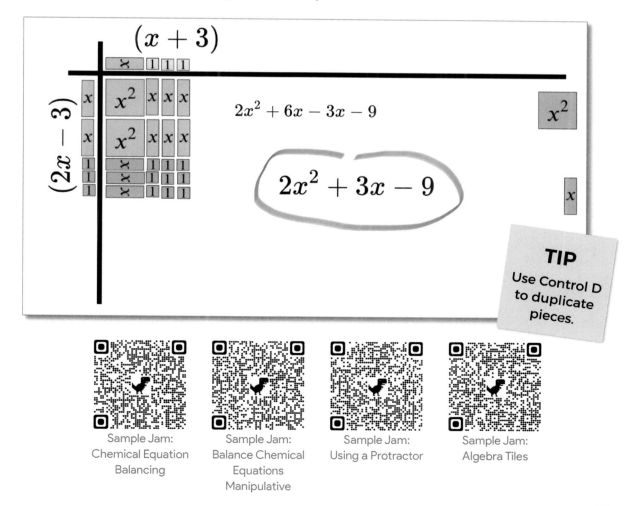

TIP
Use Control D to duplicate pieces.

Sample Jam: Chemical Equation Balancing

Sample Jam: Balance Chemical Equations Manipulative

Sample Jam: Using a Protractor

Sample Jam: Algebra Tiles

63. Enhance the Lab Experience

In a modern science class, NGSS standards ask more of the students than simply following lab procedures. They call for an active process of asking questions and designing experiments.

Jamboard is the perfect tool for students to document their learning while working on a lab or an activity. Start students off working together and making predictions in the same Jam frame using **Sticky Notes**. In another frame, students can add essential questions before starting in on their experiment design. When students dive into their experiments, they can document the process by taking pictures and making sketches in the Jam. When their results are ready, students can gather, analyze, and present information to the rest of the class.

Sample Jam: Science Walks Template

Sample Jam: What's in Your Backyard?

Sample Jam: NGSS Lab

Sample Jam: Design Process

64. Create a Timeline

Timelines can help students identify and organize information to show an order or sequence of events.

Timelines can easily be illustrated in Jamboard. Students can use the **Pen** tool to draw a timeline, use the **Shape** tool to make ticks on it, and use the **Add Image** tool to find and import supporting images. Have multiple students work together on the same Jam to research and add events to a timeline.

Sample Jam: Investments Risk Continuum by Scott Marsden

Sample Jam: Research Your Story

Sample Jam: Historical Event Timeline

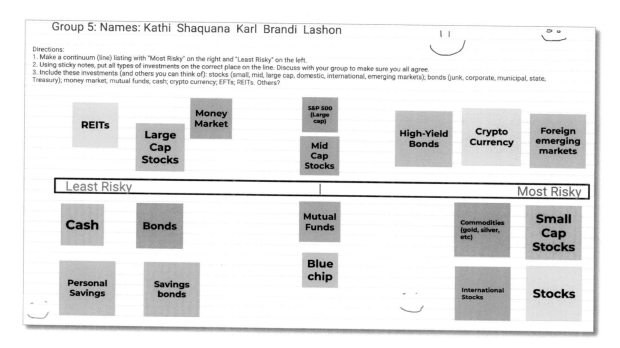

Group 5: Names: Kathi Shaquana Karl Brandi Lashon

Directions:
1. Make a continuum (line) listing with "Most Risky" on the right and "Least Risky" on the left.
2. Using sticky notes, put all types of investments on the correct place on the line. Discuss with your group to make sure you all agree.
3. Include these investments (and others you can think of): stocks (small, mid, large cap, domestic, international, emerging markets); bonds (junk, corporate, municipal, state, Treasury); money market; mutual funds; cash; crypto currency; EFTs; REITs. Others?

65. Illustrations and Animations

Illustrating ideas with moving images helps solidify concepts.

Students can model a process in a Jam. Have them create a diagram in a frame, then duplicate the frame and show how the elements of the process advance in the new frame. Duplicate and progress the frame for each step until the entire process is modeled.

TIP

It is not unusual for even a short animation to be over twenty frames.

You and your students can also create (and display) animated GIF files using Jamboard. To create an animation, start a Jam and create a diagram. The **Three Dots Icon** allows students to download the frame as an image. After downloading the frame, modify the diagram slightly and download the frame as an image again. Keep doing this until you have enough images to illustrate your idea, then upload them to a GIF maker, such as gifmaker.com, to create an animation.

For example, students might create an animation to illustrate the states of matter. They can use the **Shape** tool to illustrate the molecules and particles and the **Text Box** tool to label the phases as they change in different frames. Between frame downloads, students move the "molecules" closer together to illustrate how particles and molecules react when a substance is added.

Sample Jam: Animations with States of Matter Example

Sample Jam: Creating an Animation in Jamboard

Add an animated GIF to a Jam by using the **Add Image** tool.

66. Play with Phonics!

Jamboard is a great tool for teaching reading skills and for developing phonemic awareness.

Jamboard can illustrate sight words, letter patterns, letter sounds, vowels, consonants, and blends in a way that incorporates student interaction. Adding illustrations of phonics sounds as images or **Sticky Notes** that students can drag make different words in the frame helps students to interact with their learning.

Sample Jam:
Play with Phonics

Sample Jam:
Glued Sounds

Sample Jam:
Sight Words Bingo

TIP
Change the order of the objects so that the text is in front of any background shape.

67. The Engineering Design Process

Design is an essential process in engineering, computer science, and other STEM topics.

Illustrating the design process through multiple frames of a Jam can help students break down a project into smaller, more manageable pieces. You can also use Jamboard with STEM topics to help students stay organized, brainstorm, take notes, visualize projects, create lists, sort ideas, and much more.

Sample Jam: A-Maze-ment Movement

Sample Jam: The Engineering Design Process Template

TIP: Encourage students to use "Genius Hour"—time set aside for students to pursue passion projects—to brainstorm and identify problems within their communities.

68. Coding

Bringing coding into your classroom and connecting it with your content will allow students to have a different perspective of the lesson. It will allow them to think differently and to realize that the program will execute in the way someone wrote it.

Using coding websites, robotics, and physical computing devices, can help students make connections to what they are learning in class.

TIP
Encourage students to *design* their programs, not just code them.

Logical and computational thinking are important factors in writing successful programs.

Group students into pairs and then have each pair join a classwide Jam when thinking about what logic will work to write a program successfully. This provides everyone with the opportunity to communicate and leave feedback, and students can see the ways that others have thought differently about solutions for solving a problem.

Illustrating the plot of a story can help students with reading comprehension. Combine story and STEM, and you've got a truly engaging lesson! Use a Jam to plot a diagram for the story in one frame, then write pseudocode for a program to execute the plot in the next frame. (This is a great activity to try with Ozobot and the OzoBlockly editor.)

Sample Jam: Code the Plot

Sample Jam: Pseudocode Template

Sample Jam: App Design Task by Peter Horner

69. Icons or Emojis Story Writing

Students can use Jamboard to draft and revise story ideas using icons and emojis.

Pair students together and ask them to collaborate on a very short story in a Jam. After the first draft of writing is completed and you've given the students feedback on the story, ask the students to replace five words of the story with images.

Another writing activity that works well in a Jam is to use pictures as prompts for student stories. Put the picture on the first frame of a Jam and then have each student tell a story about it in their own frame. You might be surprised at each student's unique interpretation of the same image.

Sample Jam:
Icons, Emojis
Writing and
Prompts

Sample Jam:
Picture Prompt
Template

Sample Jam:
Image Usage
Type Jam

TIP

Use the **Three Dots Icon** on an image to duplicate it as many times as needed in the story.

70. Artistry is Awesome!

Jamboard is a great way to support communication and creativity for your students in the art classroom.

Create a Jam and insert an image of a piece of art for students to interpret directly on the Jam. Encourage them to think deeply about the object in the frame.

TIP

To prevent **Sticky Notes** and other objects from accidentally being moved, add a giant text box or transparent rectangle to the frame.

Sample Jam:
Virtual Gallery
Walk Template

Sample Jam:
Create Window
Art Template

Sample Jam:
Clear Blank
Rectangle Jam

Transparent
Rectangle Image

App Smashing

As well as supporting creativity, app smashing—working on a project in two apps together and combining the results—creates new and surprisingly intuitive ways to present information to students.

Usually when you app smash, you are combining tools together because one of the tools is lacking a feature that the other can compensate for. But combining tools can also provide a more robust and engaging activity that's greater than the sum of its parts.

The key is knowing which apps to combine.

71. Bitmoji Jams

Add your digital avatar to Jams using Bitmoji.

In order to use Bitmoji, you must download the app from the Apple Store or the Google Play Store onto your mobile device. From there, it's easy to create an account and create a digital version of yourself. Then you can download and use the Bitmoji Chrome extension in your browser to copy and paste your new Bitmoji character right into a Jam frame to express excitement or emphasize content.

TIP
Refine your Bitmoji search results in the Chrome extension with keywords like "pose," "photo," or "book."

Sample Jam:
Jamboard Tips
with Bitmoji

72. Screencastify and Jamboard Together

Pairing a screen-recording tool with Jamboard allows students or teachers to present ideas created within a Jam. After using a Jam for creative critical thinking, ask students to communicate through video.

Screencastify is a free Chrome extension that records audio and video. (Go to screencastify.com to install it on a Chromebook or PC.) You can share Screencastify video from Google Drive or export it to YouTube.

TIP
Screencastify videos automatically save to a folder in your Google Drive. Change the sharing permissions and post the video to your Google Classroom.

Sample Jam: Screencastify and Jamboard Jam

Whether you're flipping your classroom or teaching remotely, pairing Screencastify with Jamboard can help to enhance the lesson. Use it to add your voice or your face to lessons.

73. EquatIO and Jamboard

Create a better math or science Jam by integrating EquatIO with Jamboard.

EquatIO is a Chrome extension from Texthelp, the maker of Read&Write that adds math or science equations to Google apps, including Jamboard. EquatIO allows you to use your voice or handwriting recognition to insert math symbols into apps.

Clicking on the Chrome extension pops up a bar at the bottom of the screen. Choose Desmos integration to create a graph or add mathematical symbols. Export by copying the equation to your clipboard and paste the equation into the Jam.

Sample Jam: Equatio and Jamboard Jam

TIP
Change the settings in EquatIO to change the size of the image created for Jamboard.

74. Use Flipgrid to Screen Record

Flipgrid is a great (and completely free) tool for empowering students and encouraging them to use their voices.

Students can enhance their Flipgrid videos by using its screensharing features to include Jams in their topic responses. Then, their peers can view their videos and respond with their own.

Sample Jam:
Flipgrid and
Jamboard Jam

TIP
Screensharing a Jam allows camera-shy students to opt out of showing their faces in video responses.

75. Summarize Jams with Voice Typing in Slides and Docs

Google Slides, Docs, and Jamboard each have their own advantages, and they become more powerful when you use them together.

One of the advantages that Docs and Slides can lend to Jamboard is voice typing. Besides transcribing speech, the **Voice Typing** tool allows you to dictate punctuation, format text, and edit a document. In Google Slides, the dictation will appear in the speaker notes; in Google Docs it will be embedded into the document. Using the **Voice Typing** tool can assist students with accessibility needs or students who have difficulty typing.

Try having students create a collage in a Jam, which can include images or even a word cloud. Then, ask them to download the frame as an image and upload it into a Google Doc or Google Slides document and, using the **Voice Typing** tool, summarize or give their interpretations of the images.

Sample Slides:
Critique the
Reasoning of Others
with Voice Typing

Sample Jam:
Summarize Your
Jam Template

TIP
Download the voice typing template at alicekeeler.com/voicetyping to get a copy of the keyboard commands to navigate the **Voice Typing** tool.

76. Provide Feedback by Download as Image

Google apps' in-document **Comment** tool is a valuable feature that can facilitate collaboration and feedback in real time. However, at this time, Jamboard does not have this feature available. Not to worry! You can still provide in-document comments to your students by allowing them to download the frame as an image, then insert the image into a Google Slide.

Sample Jam:
Download Jam
Frame

TIP

Leave the Google team feedback about enabling comments in Jams by clicking the **Three Dots Icon** and selecting "Send feedback to Google."

Remote Learning with Jamboard

It's important to remember that remote learning is not synonymous with online classes.

For a variety of reasons, some or all of your students may not be able to be physically present in class. Jamboard supports students being able to continue to learn even when they cannot be in a classroom.

77. Social-Emotional Learning

Use Jamboard to check in with your students and ask them how they are feeling. Create a Jam for social-emotional learning (SEL) and allow your students to collaborate on it or have them complete it independently. Students can respond using the **Pen** tool, **Sticky Note** tool, **Text Box** tool, or they can even insert emojis to express their feelings.

Sample Jam:
Social-Emotional
Learning

> **TIP:** You can create an SEL assignment in Google Classroom or attach the Jam. If you select "Students can edit," they will be able to see all of the responses and collaborate together in one Jam. Alternatively, you can choose "Make a copy for each student" so that the responses are private.

78. Demonstrate a Process

A presentation tool such as Google Slides is useful for talking *to* students; Jamboard is useful for talking *with* students.

Sample Jam:
Mood Board by
Jennifer Hines

Jamboard takes lessons beyond presentation to allow the teacher to interact with the content, and it allows teachers the flexibility to adjust for student questions.

Use the **Pen** tool in the Jam to diagram and visualize a concept in response to your students' needs.

The ability to create side-by-side windows is a key skill for students using a Chromebook. Plan to take the time to work with students on getting this skill down before going deep into the curriculum. Teach students to use the **Alt and [** and **Alt and]** keyboard shortcuts to dock windows on the left, right, or side by side.

TIP

Active student engagement improves learning. Give each student a copy of a Jam so they can participate along with a demonstration.

Sample Jam: Side by Side Template

Sample Jam: Visualize Your Thinking

Sample Jam: Writing Music with Jamboard

79. Observe Student Work in Real Time

One of the challenges when working with students remotely is that it can be difficult to see student work while it is in progress.

With Jamboard, teachers monitor student progress throughout an activity or project by sharing a Jam with a student. This can be extremely helpful in determining if students understand the lesson and if they need additional support or guidance.

Sample Jam: Observe Work in Real Time Template

To do this, create an assignment in Google Classroom and attach a Jam with the "Make a copy per student" option selected, or you can have students create their own Jam and add it to the assignment. Then, you'll have access to the Jam and be able to observe their work in real time.

TIP

To access Jams quickly, click in the Class Drive folder in the Classwork page to go directly to the class folder in Drive.

80. Whiteboarding with Google Meet

While connecting with students virtually, there may be times where you need to get together to discuss concepts or a process during the lesson. Jamboard integrates right into Google Meet video conferencing.

Use the **Three Dots Icon** in Google Meet to create or open a Jam. The Jam is automatically linked in the chat, and participants are provided access. You do not need to plan in advance to use a Jam as a visual aid while working with students. The built-in Jam creation in Meet gives you quick access, and you can easily locate the meeting notes, since the Jam automatically saves to Google Drive.

At the end of the meeting, use the **Three Dots Icon** to rename the Jam with a meaningful title. If the notes are not needed, use the **Three Dots Icon** to remove (trash) the meeting Jam.

> **TIP:** Start a new Jam within Google Meet every time, even if you do not think you will use it. Once you get in the habit of having a Jam handy, the dynamics of your meetings will change to naturally incorporate visual idea-sharing.

Sample Jam:
Whiteboarding
with Google Meet

81. Magnify the Jam

You can use the **Zoom** tool in the top toolbar of a Jam to focus on a specific area of the Jam. The tool will allow you to magnify any part of the frame.

When the tool is on, the **Zoom Icon** in the toolbar turns blue, and you can click on an area of the frame to magnify it. The frame will be automatically resized, and the content will be magnified. Using this option will help keep students from being distracted.

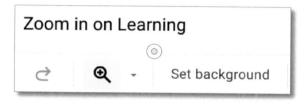

Keep in mind that the **Zoom** tool is a toggle button: when you click on the Zoom menu option, it will turn on; click on it again, and it will turn off.

> **TIP:** Holding down the **Ctrl and -** keys at the same time to zoom out makes the toolbars smaller and the frame larger. **Ctrl and 0** restores the browser zoom settings.

Sample Jam:
Zoom In on
Learning

82. Polling

Collaborating on a single Jam allows students to voice their opinions about different topics. Post questions as polls by allowing students to move a marker (an image or **Sticky Note** with their name on it) to indicate their vote.

Sample Jam:
Polling Template

TIP

Create groups of students who have voted the same way and have one of them present their position to the rest of the students. Allow them to defend their point of view to the class.

83. Use a Jam for Attendance

TIP

When students join your meet, display a welcome page that directs them to mark their attendance.

It is still important to keep track of attendance when teaching remotely. When students join your online class, share an attendance Jam with them and allow them to mark their own attendance. This should be completed during the first few minutes of each class. Keeping a consistent routine during remote instruction is important to ensure students are aware of your expectations and know their responsibilities.

At the end of the week, change the sharing permissions of the Jam to read only and make a copy of the original template for the new week. This will ensure that the attendance is not changed after the week is over.

Sample Jam:
Attendance
Template

84. Jam for Breakout Rooms

When meeting with students, you can work with small groups by utilizing the breakout rooms in your video-conferencing tool. Using breakout rooms can be extremely helpful if you want to work with a small group of students to target a skill, provide feedback, or have them work together on a task.

Explain the process and expectations to your students prior to moving them into the breakout room. Assigning student roles and responsibilities during the breakout can help you manage the entire video conference and allow you to easily circulate from room to room to ensure students are on track.

TIP

You can observe the group work in real time on the Jam without having to be in the breakout room.

Providing a Jam to each group will allow you to see the work that is being completed in real time.

Sample Jam: Breakout Room Template

Sample Jam: Breakout Room Group Template

Sample Jam: Breakout Room Group Roles Jamboard by Esther Park

85. Teach Handwriting

It's essential that young children learn to write.

Writing on paper is best for developing handwriting skills; however, when teachers and students can't be in the same space, teachers can still monitor and guide student handwriting development through Jamboard. If students are using a touchscreen Chromebook or a tablet with a stylus, they can practice forming letters using the **Pen** tool in a Jam.

> **TIP**
> Use an image with writing guidelines as a background in a Jam to help guide students in forming letters.

Sample Jam: Half-Inch Lines

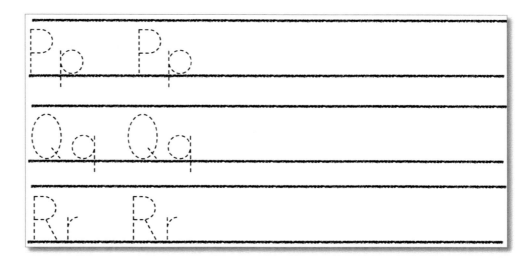

Sample Jam: Handwriting Lines

Sample Jam: Kindergarten Handwriting Lines

Sample Jam: Handwriting Lines with Name

Sample Jam: Popsicle Stick Handwriting Lines

Sample Jam: Trace Letters Jam

Going Further with the Jamboard Kiosk

It is important to remember that you do not need a Jamboard Kiosk to teach with Jamboard. However, if you do have the Kiosk, there are unique learning opportunities that you can create. We believe that someday all schools using Google for Education will invest in a Jamboard Kiosk for each teacher or classroom.

The Jamboard Kiosk is not merely an interactive whiteboard, and it does not need to be connected to a computer to work. It was designed as a collaboration tool to facilitate the sharing and recording of ideas. It was intentionally designed with a small footprint to emphasize the conversation it fosters, rather than the tool as a physical object in a classroom.

The Kiosk's stand comes at an additional cost, but it allows the Jamboard Kiosk to become mobile and be used anywhere in a school building where it can be plugged into a wall outlet—another classroom, the gym, the media center, etc. The Kiosk can be used during nonclass school events to help keep any audience engaged with conversations, content, and activities.

86. Use the Three Lines Menu

When you power on the Kiosk, it will display a new Jam that you can write on and curate information on immediately. However, if you want to save and share this Jam with your students, you must be signed into the Kiosk. After you do so, use the **Three Lines Menu** located in the upper-left corner of the Kiosk's display to save the Jam to your Drive, share the Jam with others, and open other Jams.

When you click "Save this Jam," you will be prompted to enter your email address. Your current Jam will automatically be retitled using your first name and "Jam" (e.g., "Alice Jam") and saved in your My Drive area.

> **TIP**
>
> Allow students to capture their progress by sending a copy of their Jam to their teacher. This can help track student growth and progress throughout an assignment.

Sample Jam:
The Kiosk Three
Line Menu

The "Share this Jam" option allows you to share the Jam with additional people, similar to sharing in other Google files.

"Send a Copy" will provide you the option of either sending the entire Jam file as a PDF or the current frame as an image to someone via email.

You can also choose to "Open a Jam."

87. Small-Group Collaboration

The Kiosk supports in-person learning as well as remote learning. A few students can gather together at the Kiosk to curate information while other students in the class access the Jam remotely, and work can still be completed in real time. Also, the Kiosk allows for two students to write on a frame at the same time. This is a great feature because students can be collaborating verbally while they are documenting their work. They can search the web and brainstorm ideas and solutions and insert them directly into the Jam.

Sample Jam: Small Group Collaboration on Kiosk Template 1

Sample Jam: Small Group Collaboration on Kiosk Template 2

> **TIP:** Remind students they can write, move, or resize objects with their fingers or with the passive styluses and eraser.

88. Capture the Conversation

All versions of Jamboard—the app, the web version, and the Kiosk—are great at capturing your class's conversations, but the Kiosk is the best for jumping back into them.

Sample Jam:
Open a Jam to
the Kiosk

When you power off the Kiosk and then turn it back on, Jamboard will start up back in the last Jam you were working on with students.

Though you don't have to assign an owner to a Jam on the Kiosk, it is a best practice because it allows you to store the Jam in your Drive and avoid losing the work.

> **TIP**
> Students can open their Jams to the Kiosk and share their Jam with the entire class.

89. Connect to a Global Audience

The Kiosk is ideal for connecting with expert guest speakers or making global classroom connections, allowing you to take learning far beyond

Sample Jam:
Global Connection
Template

the four walls of your classroom. Use the built-in Google Meet functionality to present a Jam to the audience that complements your out-of-class connection.

If the expert is not using Google Meet, connect your laptop or Chromebook to the Kiosk and project your screen to the Kiosk.

> **TIP**
>
> Prior to connecting with someone outside of your class, provide your students with clear expectations about etiquette and behavior.

90. Collaborate on Web Content

There are a few features in the image menu of the Kiosk that are worth mentioning.

First is the ability to search for web content or an image and insert it directly into the Jam. Although you cannot add active links to a Jam, you can use the **Crop** tool to snip the search results and include them in the Jam.

Try searching for a famous artist or object and inserting it into the Jam. Allow students to sketch their version or interpretation of it and promote a class discussion and peer review.

Another great feature is the **Sticker** menu, which provides emojis and speech-bubble stencils that can be inserted into a Jam and duplicated as needed by students or teachers.

> **TIP**
>
> The objects on the **Sticker** menu can be used to provide feedback to students while they are working.

Sample Jam:
Collaborate on
Web Content

Sample Jam:
Kiosk Collaboration
Template

Sample Jam:
Kiosk Collaboration
Example

91. Small-Station Rotation

Putting your students in small groups is a great way to promote collaboration, and having groups rotate to different small stations can really kick that up a notch. The Kiosk makes a perfect station for this kind of rotation.

Sample Jam:
Small-Station
Rotation

Students can open their Jam on the Kiosk and discuss any challenges, issues, or questions they may have with the teacher. Then, they can immediately take note of the feedback, and add or change the Jam as needed.

TIP

Catlin Tucker is an expert on blended learning who promotes the small-station-rotation model. Find out more about it at her website, catlintucker.com.

What Jamboard Adds

Education technology only works for education when it is used differently from existing tools, not as a replacement for them. Rather than thinking of Google Jamboard as an alternative for paper tasks, consider the added advantages a digital platform can offer:

- Collaboration: At least two students can be on the same Jamboard.
- Discussions: **Sticky Notes** are a new way to share ideas.
- Feedback loops: With Jamboard, students have the opportunity to respond to feedback and improve their work before being graded on it.
- Creative thinking: The open and collaborative format of Jamboard means students can make decisions together and see how different their end product looks from others'.
- Communicate ideas: Jamboard encourages students to go beyond the answer and explain their thinking.
- Get outside the class: Students can work on Jams with others who are not in the same place or who are working at different times.
- Gamify learning: Jamboard promotes engagement through fun.

Acknowledgments

We'd like to thank the following individuals:

- Barton Keeler
- Jim Mattina
- Alexes Terry of Twisted Teaching
- Esther Park
- Scott Marsden
- Holly Clark
- Gavin Mattina
- Wes Force
- Peter Horner
- Brigid Duncan
- Jennifer Hines
- Kristen Longstaff
- Irina Ostrovskaya
- Galloway Township school district

About the Authors

Alice Keeler

 @alicekeeler

Alice Keeler is a mom of five children and a global leader in educational technology. She has taught high school mathematics since 1999, mostly 1:1, and taught in the teacher-credential program at California State University, Fresno. She holds a bachelor's degree in mathematics and a master's degree in educational media design and technology and is a Google Certified Innovator and Google Apps Script Developer. She has worked on projects such as YouTube for Teachers, Google Applied Digital Skills, Google Play for Education, and Bing in the Classroom, and she's the founder of coffeeEDU.

Teaching with Google Jamboard is the seventh book that Alice has co-authored. Others include *50 Things to Go Further with Google Classroom* and *Ditch That Homework*. She frequently blogs on teaching with G Suite at **alicekeeler.com**.

Kimberly Mattina

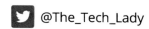 @The_Tech_Lady

Kimberly Mattina is a wife, mother, daughter, educator, and lifelong learner. She is a full-time technology teacher in New Jersey and has been an educator for fifteen years. Her main focus is teaching technology/STEM integration and computer science.

She is a Google Certified Trainer and Educator; Gold Product Expert; Google Educator Group Leader for NJ; GEG Mentor; and ambassador for Ozobot, WeVideo, BookCreator, and Wakelet.

In addition, Kimberly is the host of The Suite Talk, a show and podcast about connecting and helping educators around the world to integrate technology effectively in the classroom. Visit thesuitetalk.com for more information.

More from DaveBurgess Consulting, Inc.

Since 2012, DBCI has been publishing books that inspire and equip educators to be their best. For more information on our titles or to purchase bulk orders for your school, district, or book study, visit **DaveBurgessConsulting.com/DBCIbooks**.

MORE TEACHING METHODS & MATERIALS

All 4s and 5s by Andrew Sharos

Boredom Busters by Katie Powell

The Classroom Chef by John Stevens and Matt Vaudrey

The Collaborative Classroom by Trevor Muir

Copyrighteous by Diana Gill

CREATE by Bethany J. Petty

Ditch That Homework by Matt Miller and Alice Keeler

Ditch That Textbook by Matt Miller

Don't Ditch That Tech by Matt Miller, Nate Ridgway, and Angelia Ridgway

EDrenaline Rush by John Meehan

Educated by Design by Michael Cohen, the Tech Rabbi

The EduProtocol Field Guide by Marlena Hebern and Jon Corippo

The EduProtocol Field Guide: Book 2 by Marlena Hebern and Jon Corippo

The EduProtocol Field Guide: Math Edition by Lisa Nowakowski and Jeremiah Ruesch

Expedition Science by Becky Schnekser

Game On? Brain On! by Lindsay Portnoy, PhD

Guided Math AMPED by Reagan Tunstall

Innovating Play by Jessica LaBar-Twomy and Christine Pinto

Instant Relevance by Denis Sheeran

LAUNCH by John Spencer and A.J. Juliani

Make Learning MAGICAL by Tisha Richmond

Pass the Baton by Kathryn Finch and Theresa Hoover

Project-Based Learning Anywhere by Lori Elliott

Pure Genius by Don Wettrick

The Revolution by Darren Ellwein and Derek McCoy

Shift This! by Joy Kirr

Skyrocket Your Teacher Coaching by Michael Cary Sonbert

Spark Learning by Ramsey Musallam

Sparks in the Dark by Travis Crowder and Todd Nesloney

Table Talk Math by John Stevens

Unpack Your Impact by Naomi O'Brien and
  LaNesha Tabb

The Wild Card by Hope and Wade King

The Writing on the Classroom Wall by
  Steve Wyborney

You Are Poetry by Mike Johnston

LIKE A PIRATETM SERIES

Teach Like a PIRATE by Dave Burgess

eXPlore Like a PIRATE by Michael Matera

Learn Like a PIRATE by Paul Solarz

Play Like a PIRATE by Quinn Rollins

Run Like a PIRATE by Adam Welcome

Tech Like a PIRATE by Matt Miller

LEAD LIKE A PIRATETM SERIES

Lead Like a PIRATE by Shelley Burgess and
  Beth Houf

Balance Like a PIRATE by Jessica Cabeen, Jessica
  Johnson, and Sarah Johnson

Lead beyond Your Title by Nili Bartley

Lead with Appreciation by Amber Teamann and
  Melinda Miller

Lead with Culture by Jay Billy

Lead with Instructional Rounds by Vicki Wilson

Lead with Literacy by Mandy Ellis

LEADERSHIP & SCHOOL CULTURE

Beyond the Surface of Restorative Practices by
  Marisol Rerucha

Choosing to See by Pamela Seda and Kyndall Brown

Culturize by Jimmy Casas

Escaping the School Leader's Dunk Tank by Rebecca
  Coda and Rick Jetter

Fight Song by Kim Bearden

From Teacher to Leader by Starr Sackstein

If the Dance Floor Is Empty, Change the Song by
  Joe Clark

The Innovator's Mindset by George Couros

It's OK to Say "They" by Christy Whittlesey

Kids Deserve It! by Todd Nesloney and
  Adam Welcome

Let Them Speak by Rebecca Coda and Rick Jetter

The Limitless School by Abe Hege and Adam Dovico

Live Your Excellence by Jimmy Casas

Next-Level Teaching by Jonathan Alsheimer

The Pepper Effect by Sean Gaillard

Principaled by Kate Barker, Kourtney Ferrua, and
  Rachael George

The Principled Principal by Jeffrey Zoul and
  Anthony McConnell

Relentless by Hamish Brewer

The Secret Solution by Todd Whitaker, Sam Miller,
  and Ryan Donlan

Start. Right. Now. by Todd Whitaker, Jeffrey Zoul, and
  Jimmy Casas

Stop. Right. Now. by Jimmy Casas and Jeffrey Zoul

Teachers Deserve It by Rae Hughart and Adam
  Welcome

Teach Your Class Off by CJ Reynolds

They Call Me "Mr. De" by Frank DeAngelis

Thrive through the Five by Jill M. Siler

Unmapped Potential by Julie Hasson and
  Missy Lennard

When Kids Lead by Todd Nesloney and Adam Dovico

Word Shift by Joy Kirr

Your School Rocks by Ryan McLane and Eric Lowe

TECHNOLOGY & TOOLS

50 Things You Can Do with Google Classroom by Alice
  Keeler and Libbi Miller

50 Things to Go Further with Google Classroom by
  Alice Keeler and Libbi Miller

INSPIRATION, PROFESSIONAL GROWTH & PERSONAL DEVELOPMENT

CHILDREN'S BOOKS

Beyond Us by Aaron Polansky

Cannonball In by Tara Martin

Dolphins in Trees by Aaron Polansky

I Want to Be a Lot by Ashley Savage

The Princes of Serendip by Allyson Apsey

Ride with Emilio by Richard Nares

The Wild Card Kids by Hope and Wade King

Zom-Be a Design Thinker by Amanda Fox

Made in the USA
Middletown, DE
17 June 2021